STREETS IN TIMGAD.
From a photograph.

FRONTISPIECE.

# ANCIENT TOWN-PLANNING

# ANCIENT TOWN-PLANNING

By

F. HAVERFIELD

GYAN

*Published by*

Gyan Publishing House
5, Ansari Road
Daryaganj, New Delhi-110002
Phone: 011-47034999, 9811692060
E-mail: books@gyanbooks.com

*Distribution Network*
gyanbooks.com
India, USA, Canada, UK, Australia, France



ISBN : 978-81-212-6482-2 (PB)
First Published, 1913

2nd Impression 2022

*Printed at:* Gyan Press, Delhi.



**ANCIENT TOWN-PLANNING**
Author: F. HAVERFIELD

# ANCIENT TOWN-PLANNING

BY

F. HAVERFIELD

1913

# PREFACE

THE following pages are an enlargement of a paper read to the University of London as the Creighton Lecture for 1910, and also submitted in part to the London Conference on Town-planning in the same year.

The original lecture was written as a scholar's contribution to a modern movement. It looked on town-planning as one of those new methods of social reform, which stand in somewhat sharp contrast with the usual aims of political parties and parliaments. The latter concern mainly the outward and public life of men as fellow-citizens in a state; they involve such problems as Home Rule, Disestablishment, Protection. The newer ideals centre round the daily life of human beings in their domestic environment. Men and women —or rather, women and men—have begun to demand that the health and housing and food and comfort of mankind, and much else that not long ago seemed to lie outside the scope of legislation, should be treated with as close attention and logic and intelligence as any of the older and more conventional problems of politicians. They will not leave even the tubes of babies' feeding-bottles to an off-hand opportunism.

Among these newer efforts town-planning is one

of the better known. Most of us now admit that if some scores of dwellings have to be run up for working-men or city-clerks—or even for University teachers in North Oxford—they can and should be planned with regard to the health and convenience and occupations of their probable tenants. Town-planning has taken rank as an art; it is sometimes styled a science and University professorships are named after it; in the London Conference of 1910 it got its *deductio in forum* or at least its first dance. But it is still young and its possibilities undefined. Its name is apt to be applied to all sorts of building-schemes, and little attempt is made to assign it any specific sense. It is only slowly making its way towards the recognized method and the recognized principles which even an art requires. Here, it seemed, a student of ancient history might proffer parallels from antiquity, and especially from the Hellenistic and Roman ages, which somewhat resemble the present day in their care for the well-being of the individual.

In enlarging the lecture I have tried not only to preserve this point of view, but also to treat the subject in a manner useful to classical scholars and historians. The details of Greek and Roman town-planning are probably little known to many who study Greek and Roman life, and though they have often been incidentally discussed,[1] they have never been collected. The

[1] For example, by Beloch in his volume on the cities of Campania, by Schulten in various essays, by Barthel in a recent inquiry into

material, however, is plentiful, and it illuminates vividly the character and meaning of that city-life which, in its different forms, was a vital element in both the Greek and the Roman world. Even our little towns of Silchester and Caerwent in Roman Britain become more intelligible by its aid. The Roman student gains perhaps more than the Hellenist from this inquiry, since the ancient Roman builder planned more regularly and the modern Roman archaeologist has dug more widely. But admirable German excavations at Priene, Miletus, and elsewhere declare that much may be learnt about Greek towns and in Greek lands.

The task of collecting and examining these details is not easy. It needs much local knowledge and many local books, all of which are hard to come by. Here, as in most branches of Roman history, we want a series of special inquiries into the fortunes of individual Roman towns in Italy and the provinces, carried out by men who combine two things which seldom go together, scientific and parochial knowledge. But a body of evidence already waits to be used, and though its discussion may lead—as it has led me—into topographical minutiae, where completeness and certainty are too often unattainable and errors are fatally easy, my results may nevertheless contain some new suggestions and may help some future workers.

Roman Africa, and by others, to be cited below. Dr. J. Stübben in his *Städtebau* (Darmstadt, ed. 2, 1907) and Mr. Raymond Unwin in his *Town planning in practice* (London, 1909) have given interesting notices and illustrations of the subject for modern builders.

I have avoided technical terms as far as I could, and that not merely in the interests of the general reader. Such terms are too often both ugly and unnecessary. When a foreign scholar writes of a Roman town as 'scamnirt' or 'strigirt', it is hard to avoid the feeling that this is neither pleasant nor needful. Perhaps it is not even accurate, as I shall point out below. I have accordingly tried to make my text as plain as possible and to confine technicalities to the footnotes.

F. H.

# CONTENTS

# LIST OF PLANS AND ILLUSTRATIONS

(For precise references to sources see the various footnotes.)

For the loan of blocks I am indebted to the Académie des Inscriptions et Belles-Lettres (fig. 21), to the German Imperial Archaeological Institute (fig. 9), to the Royal Geographical Society (fig. 36), and to the Royal Institute of British Architects and the Editors of the *Transactions of the Town-Planning Conference*, 1911 (figs. 7, 8, 17, 30, 32, 35). Fig. 11 is from Mr. T. E. Peet's *Stone and Bronze Ages in Italy*. The other 26 blocks have been prepared for this volume.

# TABLE OF MEASURES

THE following figures may be found convenient by readers who wish to take special account of the dimensions cited in the following pages, and may also help them to correct any errors which I have unwittingly admitted.

1 Roman foot = 0·296 metres = 0·97 English feet. For practical purposes 100 Roman feet = 97 English feet.

1 Iugerum = 120 × 240 Roman feet = 116·4 × 233·8 English feet. For practical purposes a *Iugerum* may be taken to be rather over $\frac{2}{3}$ of an acre and rather over $\frac{1}{4}$ of a hectare, and more exactly 2523·3 sq. metres.

1 Metre = 1·09 English yards, a trifle less than 40 ins. 402·5 metres equal a quarter of a mile.

1 Hectare (10000 sq. metres) = 2·47 acres (11955 sq. yds.).

1 Acre = nearly $69\frac{1}{2} \times 69\frac{1}{2}$ yds. (208·7 ft. square) = 4840 sq. yds.

# CHAPTER I

## Preliminary Remarks

Town-planning—the art of laying out towns with due care for the health and comfort of inhabitants, for industrial and commercial efficiency, and for reasonable beauty of buildings—is an art of intermittent activity. It belongs to special ages and circumstances. For its full unfolding two conditions are needed. The age must be one in which, whether through growth or through movements of population, towns are being freely founded or freely enlarged, and almost as a matter of course attention is drawn to methods of arranging and laying out such towns. And secondly, the builders of these towns must have wit enough to care for the well-being of common men and the due arrangement of ordinary dwellings. That has not always happened. In many lands and centuries—in ages where civilization has been tinged by an undercurrent of barbarism—one or both of these conditions have been absent. In Asia during much of its history, in early Greece, in Europe during the first half of the Middle Ages, towns have consisted of one or two dominant buildings, temple or church or castle, of one or two processional avenues for worshippers at sacred festivals, and a little adjacent chaos of tortuous lanes and squalid houses. Architects have devised beautiful buildings in such towns. But they have not touched the chaos or treated the whole inhabited area as one unit. Town-planning has been here unknown.[1]

In other periods towns have been founded in large numbers and full-grown or nearly full-grown, to furnish homes for multitudes of common men, and their founders have built them on some plan or system. One such period is, of course, our own. Within the last half-century towns have arisen all over Europe and America. They are many in number. They are large in area. Most of them have been born almost full-grown; some have been established complete; others have developed abruptly out of small villages; elsewhere, additions huge enough to form separate cities have sprung up beside towns already great. Throughout this development we can trace a tendency to plan, beginning with the unconscious mechanical arrangements of industrial cities or suburbs and ending in the conscious efforts of to-day.

If we consider their size and their number together, these new European and American towns surpass anything that the world has yet seen. But, save in respect of size, the process of founding or enlarging towns is no new thing. In the old world, alike in the Greek lands round the eastern Mediterranean and in the wide empire of Rome, urban life increased rapidly at certain periods through the establishment of towns almost full-grown. The earliest towns of Greece and Italy were,

[1] Compare Brinckmann's remarks on mediaeval towns: 'Der Nachdruck liegt auf den einzelnen Gebäuden, der Kathedrale, dem Palazzo publico, den festen Palästen des Adels, nicht auf ihrer einheitlichen Verbindung. Ebenso erscheint die ganze Stadt nur eine Ansammlung einzelner Bauten. Strassen und Plätze sind unbebaute Reste.'

through sheer necessity, small. They could not grow beyond the steep hill-tops which kept them safe, or house more inhabitants than their scanty fields could feed.[1] But the world was then large; new lands lay open to those who had no room at home, and bodies of willing exiles, keeping still their custom of civil life, planted new towns throughout the Mediterranean lands. The process was extended by state aid. Republics or monarchs founded colonies to extend their power or to house their veterans, and the results were equally towns springing up full-grown in southern Europe and western Asia and even northern Africa. So too in remoter regions. Obscure evidence from China suggests that there also in early times towns were planted and military colonies were sent to outlying regions on somewhat the same methods as were used by the Greeks and Romans.

Even under less kindly conditions, the art has not been wholly dormant. Special circumstances or special men have called it into brief activity. The 'bastides' and the 'villes neuves' of thirteenth-century France were founded at a particular period and under special circumstances, and, brief as the period was and governed by military urgencies, they were laid out on a more or less definite plan (p. 143). The streets designed by Wood at Bath about 1735, by Craig at Edinburgh about 1770, by Grainger at Newcastle about 1835,

[1] For the connexion between such towns and their local food-supply, note the story of Alexander the Great and the architect Dinocrates told by Vitruvius (II. i). Dinocrates had planned a new town; Alexander asked if there were lands round it to supply it with corn, and on hearing there were none, at once ruled out the proposed site.

show what individual genius could do at favourable moments. But such instances, however interesting in themselves, are obviously less important than the larger manifestations of town-planning in Greece and Rome.

In almost all cases, the frequent establishment of towns has been accompanied by the adoption of a definite principle of town-planning, and throughout the principle has been essentially the same. It has been based on the straight line and the right angle. These, indeed, are the marks which sunder even the simplest civilization from barbarism. The savage, inconsistent in his moral life, is equally inconsistent, equally unable to 'keep straight', in his house-building and his road-making. Compare, for example, a British and a Roman road. The Roman road ran proverbially direct; even its few curves were not seldom formed by straight lines joined together. The British road was quite different. It curled as fancy dictated, wandered along the foot or the scarp of a range of hills, followed the ridge of winding downs, and only by chance stumbled briefly into straightness. Whenever ancient remains show a long straight line or several correctly drawn right angles, we may be sure that they date from a civilized age.

In general, ancient town-planning used not merely the straight line and the right angle but the two together. It tried very few experiments involving other angles. Once or twice, as at Rhodes (pp. 31, 81), we hear of streets radiating fan-fashion from a common centre, like the gangways of an ancient theatre or the thoroughfares of modern Karlsruhe, or that Palma Nuova, founded by Venice in 1593 to defend its north-eastern boundaries, which was shaped almost like a starfish. But, as a rule, the streets ran parallel or at right angles to each other and the blocks of houses which they enclosed were either square or oblong.

Much variety is noticeable, however, in details. Sometimes the outline of the ancient town was square or almost square, the house-blocks were of the same shape, and the plan of the town was indistinguishable from a chess-board. Or, instead of squares, oblong house-blocks formed a pattern not strictly that of a chess-board but geometrical and rectangular. Often the outline of the town was irregular and merely convenient, but the streets still kept, so far as they could, to a rectangular plan. Sometimes, lastly, the rectangular planning was limited to a few broad thoroughfares, while the smaller side-streets were utterly irregular. Other variations may be seen in the prominence granted or refused to public and especially to sacred buildings. In some towns full provision was made for these; ample streets with stately vistas led up to them, and open spaces were left from which they could be seen with advantage. In others there were neither vistas nor open spaces nor even splendid buildings.

A measure of historical continuity can be traced in the occurrence of these variations. The towns of the earlier Greeks were stately enough in their public buildings and principal thoroughfares, but they revealed a half-barbaric spirit in their mean side-streets and unlovely dwellings. In the middle of the fifth century men rose above this ideal. They began to recognize private houses and to attempt an adequate grouping of their cities as units capable of a single plan. But they did not carry this conception very far. The decorative still dominated the useful. Broad straight streets were still few and were laid out mainly as avenues for processions and as ample spaces for great façades.[1] Private houses were still of small account. The notion that the City was the State, helpful and progressive as it was, did something also to paralyse in certain ways the development of cities.

A change came with the new philosophy and the new politics of the Macedonian era. The older Greek City-states had been large, wealthy, and independent; magnificent buildings and sumptuous festivals were as natural to them as to the greater autonomous municipalities in all ages. But in the Macedonian period the individual cities sank to be parts of a larger whole, items in a dominant state, subjects of military monarchies. The use of public buildings, the splendour of public festivals in individual cities, declined. Instead, the claims of the individual citizen, neglected too much by the City-states but noted by the newer philosophy, found consideration even in town-planning. A more definite, more symmetrical, often more rigidly 'chess-board' pattern was introduced for the towns which now began to be founded in many countries round and east of the Aegean. Ornamental edifices and broad streets were still indeed included, but in the house-blocks round them due space and place were left for the dwellings of common men. For a while the Greeks turned their

[1] Pindar mentions 'the paved road cut straight to be smitten by horse-hoofs in processions of men that besought Apollo's care' at Cyrene (*Pyth.* v. 90). An inscription from the Piraeus, of 320 B.C., orders the Agoranomi (p. 37) to take care 'of the broad roads by which the processions move to the temple of Zeus the Saviour'.

minds to those details of daily life which in their greater age they had somewhat ignored.

Lastly, the town-planning of the Macedonian era combined, as I believe, with other and Italian elements and formed the town system of the later Roman Republic and the Roman Empire. As in art and architecture, so also in city-planning, the civilization of Greece and of Italy merged almost inextricably into a result which, with all its Greek affinities, is in the end Roman. The student now meets a rigidity of street-plan and a conception of public buildings which are neither Greek nor Oriental. The Roman town was usually a rectangle broken up into four more or less equal and rectangular parts by two main streets which crossed at right angles at or near its centre. To these two streets all the other streets ran parallel or at right angles, and there resulted a definite 'chess-board' pattern of rectangular house-blocks (*insulae*), square or oblong in shape, more or less uniform in size. The streets themselves were moderate in width; even the main thoroughfares were little wider than the rest, and the public buildings within the walls were now merged in the general mass of houses. The chief structure, the Forum, was an enclosed court, decorated indeed by statues and girt with colonnades, but devoid of façades which could dominate a town. The town councils of the Roman world were no more free than those of Greece or modern England from the municipal vice of over-building. But they had not the same openings for error. On the other hand, there was in most of them a good municipal supply of water, and sewers were laid beneath their streets.

The reason for all this is plain. These Roman towns, even more than the Greek cities of the Macedonian world, were parts of a greater whole. They were items in the Roman Empire; their citizens were citizens of Rome. They had neither the wealth nor the wish to build vast temples or public halls or palaces, such as the Greeks constructed. Their greatest edifices, the theatre and the amphitheatre, witness to the prosperity and population not so much of single towns as of whole neighbourhoods which flocked in to periodic performances.[1] But these towns had unity. Their various parts were, in some sense, harmonized, none being neglected and none grievously over-indulged, and the whole was treated as one organism. Despite limitations which are obvious, the Roman world made a more real sober and consistent attempt to plan towns than any previous age had witnessed.

[1] Compare the crowd of Nucerians who made a riot in the amphitheatre at Pompeii in A.D. 59 (Tac. *Ann.* xiv. 17). The common idea that the population of a town can be calculated by the number of seats in its theatre or amphitheatre is quite amiss.

## CHAPTER II

### GREEK TOWN-PLANNING. THE ORIGINS, BABYLON

THE beginnings of ideas and institutions are seldom well known or well recorded. They are necessarily insignificant and they win scant notice from contemporaries. Town-planning has fared like the rest. Early forms of it appear in Greece during the fourth and fifth centuries B.C.; the origin of these forms is obscure. The oldest settlement of man in town fashion which has yet been explored in any land near Greece is that of Kahun, in Egypt, dating from about 2500 B.C. Here Professor Flinders Petrie unearthed many four-roomed cottages packed close in parallel oblong blocks and a few larger rectangular houses : they are (it seems) the dwellings of the workmen and managers busy with the neighbouring Illahun pyramid.[1] But the settlement is very small, covering less than 20 acres; it is not in itself a real town and its plan has not the scheme or symmetry of a town-plan. For that we must turn to western Asia, to Babylonia and Assyria.

Here we find clearer evidence. The great cities of the Mesopotamian plains show faint traces of town-planning datable to the eighth and following centuries, of which the Greeks seem to have heard and which they may have copied. Our knowledge of these cities is, of course,

[1] W. F. Petrie, *Illahun, Kahun, and Gurob* (London, 1891), ch. ii, plate xiv. The plan is reproduced in Breasted's *History of Egypt*, p. 87, R. Unwin's *Town planning*, fig. 11 (with wrong scale), &c.

still very fragmentary, and though it has been much widened by the latest German excavations, it does not yet carry us to definite conclusions. The evidence is twofold, in part literary, drawn from Greek writers and above all Herodotus, and in part archaeological, yielded by Assyrian and Babylonian ruins.

The description of Babylon given by Herodotus is, of course, famous.[1] Even in his own day, it was well enough known to be parodied by contemporary comedians in the Athenian theatre. Probably it rests in part on first-hand knowledge. Herodotus gives us to understand that he visited Babylon in the course of his many wanderings and we have no cause to distrust him; we may even date his visit to somewhere about 450 B.C. He was not indeed the only Greek of his day, nor the first, to get so far afield. But his account nevertheless neither is nor professes to be purely that of an eyewitness. Like other writers in various ages,[2] he drew no sharp division between details which he saw and details which he learnt from others. For the sake (it may be) of vividness, he sets them all on one plane, and they must be judged, not as first-hand evidence but on their own merits.

Babylon, says Herodotus, was planted in an open plain and formed an exact square of great size, 120 stades (that is, nearly 14 miles) each way; the whole circuit was 480 stades, about 55 miles. It was girt with immense brick walls, 340 ft. high and

[1] Hdt. i. 178 foll. The accounts of Ctesias and other ancient writers seem to throw no light on the town-planning and streets of Babylon, however useful they may otherwise be.

[2] The Elizabethan description of Britain by William Harrison is an example from a modern time.

nearly 90 ft. thick, and a broad deep moat full of water, and was entered through 100 gates; presumably we are intended to think of these gates as arranged symmetrically, 25 in each side. From corner to corner the city was cut diagonally by the Euphrates, which thus halved it into two roughly equal triangles, and the river banks were fortified by brick defences—less formidable than the main outer walls—which ran along them from end to end of the city. There was, too, an inner wall on the landward side. The streets were also remarkable:

'The city itself (he says) is full of houses, three or four storeys high, and has been laid out with its streets straight, notably those which run at right angles, that is, those which lead to the river. Each road runs to a small gate in the brick river-wall: there are as many gates as lanes.'[1]

In each part of the city (that is, on either bank of the Euphrates) were specially large buildings, in one part the royal palaces, in the other the temple of Zeus Belos, bronze-gated, square in outline, 400 yards in breadth and length.

So far, in brief, Herodotus. Clearly his words suggest town-planning. The streets that ran straight and the others that ran at right angles are significant enough, even though we may doubt exactly what is meant by these other streets and what they met or cut

[1] Hdt. i. 180 *τὸ δὲ ἄστυ αὐτό, ἐὸν πλῆρες οἰκιέων τριωρόφων τε καὶ τετρωρόφων, κατατέτμηται τὰς ὁδοὺς ἰθέας, τάς τε ἄλλας καὶ τὰς ἐπικαρσίας, τὰς ἐπὶ τὸν ποταμὸν ἐχούσας.* Apparently *ἐπικαρσίας* means, as Stein says, those at right angles to the general course of the river, but this nearly = at right angles to the other roads. The course of the river appears to have been straighter then than it is now.

at right angles. But his account cannot be accepted as it stands. Whatever he saw and whatever his accuracy of observation and memory, not all of his story can be true. His Babylon covers nearly 200 square miles; its walls are over 50 miles long and 30 yds. thick and all but 120 yds. high; its gates are a mile and a half apart. The area of London to-day is no more than 130 square miles, and the topmost point of St. Paul's is barely 130 yds. high. Nanking is the largest city-site in China and its walls are the work of an Empire greater than Babylon; but they measure less than 24 miles in circuit, and they are or were little more than 30 ft. thick and 70 ft. high.[1] Moreover, Herodotus's account of the walls has to be set beside a statement which he makes elsewhere, that they had been razed by Darius sixty or seventy years before his visit.[2] The destruction can hardly have been complete. But in any case Herodotus can only have seen fragments, easily misinterpreted, easily explained by local *ciceroni* as relics of something quite unlike the facts.

Turn now to the actual remains of Babylon, as known from surveys and excavations. We find a large district extending to both banks of the Euphrates, which is covered rather irregularly by the mounds

[1] L. Gaillard, *Variétés sinologiques*, xvi (plan) and xxiii. pp. 8, 235 (Chang-hai, 1898, 1903). Others give the figures a little differently, but not so as to affect the argument.

[2] Hdt. iii. 159. The theory that there were originally two parallel outer walls, that Darius razed one and Herodotus saw the other (Baumstark in Pauly-Wissowa, *Real-Encycl.* ii. 2696), is meaningless. There could be no use in razing one and leaving the other, which was almost as strong (Hdt. i. 181). It is, however, not quite certain that Herodotus (i. 181) meant that there were two outer parallel walls.

of many ruined buildings. Two sites in it are especially notable. At its southern end is Birs Nimrud and some adjacent mounds, anciently Borsippa; here stood a huge temple of the god Nebo. Near its north end, ten or eleven miles north of Borsippa, round Babil and Kasr, is a larger wilderness of ruin, three miles long and nearly as broad in extreme dimensions; here town-walls and palaces of Babylonian kings and temples of Babylonian gods and streets and dwelling-houses of ordinary men have been detected and in part uncovered. Other signs of inhabitation can be traced elsewhere in this district, as yet unexplored.

Not unnaturally, some scholars have thought that this whole region represents the ancient Babylon and that the vast walls of Herodotus enclosed it all.[1] This view, however, cannot be accepted. Quite apart from the considerations urged above, the region in question is not square but rather triangular, and traces of wall and ditch surrounding it are altogether wanting, though city-walls have survived elsewhere in this neighbourhood and though nothing can wholly delete an ancient ditch. We have, in short, no good reason to believe that Babylon, in any form or sense whatever, covered at any time this large area.

On the other hand, the special ruins of Babil and Kasr and adjacent mounds seem to preserve both the name and the actual remains of Babylon (fig. 1). Here, on the left bank of the Euphrates, are vast city-walls, once five or six miles long.[2] They may be described roughly

[1] So Baumstark, art. Babylon in Pauly-Wissowa, ii. 2696.

[2] F. H. Weissbach, *Stadtbild von Babylon* (*Der alte Orient*, fasc. 5); R. Koldewey, *Tempel von Babylon und Borsippa*, plates i, ii; S. Langdon, *Expositor*, 1909, pp. 82, 142; Hommel, *Geogr. des alten Orients*,

as enclosing half of a square bisected diagonally by the river, much as Herodotus writes; there is good reason to think that they had some smaller counterpart on the right bank, as yet scantily explored. Within these walls were the palaces of the Babylonian kings, Nabopolassar and Nebuchadnezzar (625–561 B.C.), the temples of the national god Marduk or Merodach and

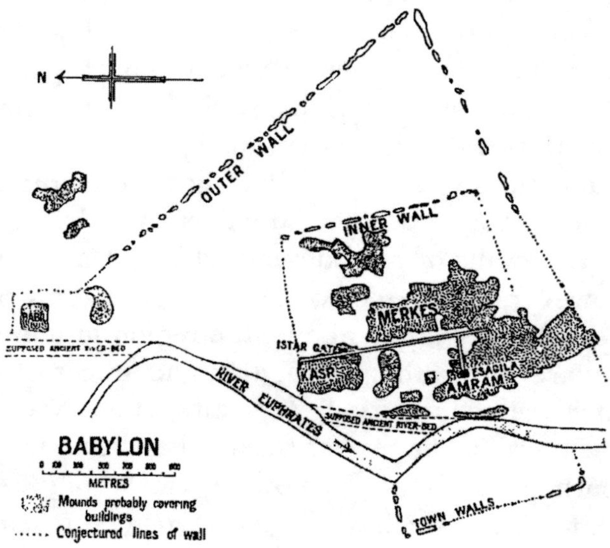


FIG. 1. (After Koldewey and others.)

other Babylonian deities, a broad straight road, Aiburschabu, running north and south from palaces to temples, a stately portal spanning this road at the Istar Gate, many private houses in the Merkes

pp. 290, 331; E. Meyer, *Sitzungsber. preuss. Akad.* 1912, p. 1102. I am indebted to Dr. Langdon for references to some of the treatises cited here and below. I cannot share the unfavourable view which is taken by Messrs. How and Wells, the latest good editors of Herodotus, of the views of these writers.

quarter, and an inner town-wall perhaps of earlier date. Street and gate were built or rebuilt by Nebuchadnezzar. He, as he declares in various inscriptions, 'paved the causeway with limestone flags for the procession of the Great Lord Marduk.' He made the Istar Gate 'with glazed brick and placed on its threshold colossal bronze bulls and ferocious serpent dragons'. Along the street thus built the statue of Marduk was borne in solemn march on the Babylonian New Year's Day, when the king paid yearly worship to the god of his country.[1]

Such are the remains of the city of Babylon, so far as they are known at present. They do not fit ill with the words of Herodotus. We can detect in them the semblance not indeed of one square but of two unequal half-squares, divided by the river; we can trace at least one great street parallel to the river and others which run at right angles to it towards the river. If the brick defences along the water-side have vanished, that may be due to their less substantial character and to the many changes of the river itself. To the student of Babylonian topography, the account of Herodotus is of very little worth. But it is as good as most modern travellers could compile, if they were let loose in a vast area of buildings, without plans, without instruments, and without any notion that a scientific description was expected of them.

The remains show also—and this is more to our purpose—the idea of the sacred processional avenue which recurs in fifth-century Greece—and is indeed

[1] Koldewey, *Pflastersteine von Aiburschabu* (Leipzig, 1901). Some of the streets of Babylon are much older than 600 B.C., but this point needs to be worked out further.

beloved of architects in the most modern times. Here is a germ of town-planning. But whether this laying out of streets extended beyond the main highways, is less clear. The Merkes excavations occasionally show streets meeting at right angles and at least one roughly rectangular *insula*, of 150 × 333 ft. But the adjoining house-blocks agree neither in size nor shape, and no hint seems to have yet come to light of a true chess-board pattern.[1]

A little further evidence can be drawn from other Mesopotamian sites. The city of Asshur had a long, broad avenue like the sacred road of Babylon, but the one *insula* of its private houses which has yet been excavated, planned and published, shows no sign of rectangular planning.[2] There is also literary evidence that Sanherib (765–681 B.C.) laid out a 'Kingsway' 100 ft. wide to promote easy movement through his city of Nineveh, and Delitzsch has even credited the Sargonid dynasty generally (722–625 B.C.) with a care for the dwellings of common men as well as of gods and of kings.[3]

In conclusion, the mounds of Babil and Kasr and others near them seem to represent the Babylon alike of fact and of Herodotus. It was a smaller city than the Greek historian avers; its length and breadth were nearer four than fourteen miles. But it had at least one straight, ample, and far-stretching highway which gave space for the ceremonies and the processions, if not

[1] *Mitteilungen der deutschen Orient-Gesellschaft* 42, Dec. 1909, pp. 7, 19; 44, Dec. 1910, p. 26.

[2] *Mitt. deutsch. Orient-Gesell.* 28, Sept. 1905; 31, May 1906.

[3] F. Delitzsch, *Asurbanipal und die assyr. Kultur seiner Zeit* (*Der alte Orient*, Leipzig, 1909), p. 25.

for the business or the domestic comforts, of life. In a sense at least, it was laid out with its streets straight. Nor was it the only city of such a kind in the Mesopotamian region. Asshur and Nineveh, both of them somewhat earlier in date than Babylon, possessed similar features. These towns, or at least Babylon, seem to have been known to Greek travellers, and probably suggested to them the adornment of their Hellenic homes with similar streets. The germ of Greek town-planning came from the east.

# CHAPTER III

## Greek Town-planning: First Efforts

Greek town-planning began in the great age of Greece, the fifth century B.C. But that age had scant sympathy for such a movement, and its beginnings were crude and narrow. Before the middle of the century the use of the processional highway had established itself in Greece. Rather later, a real system of town-planning, based on streets that crossed at right angles, became known and practised. Later still, in the early fourth century, the growing care for town-life produced town by-laws and special magistrates to execute them. In some form or other, town-planning had now taken root in the Greek world.

The two chief cities of Greece failed, indeed, to welcome the new movement. Both Athens, the city which by itself means Greece to most of us, and Sparta, the rival of Athens, remained wholly untouched by it. Alike in the days of Themistocles and Pericles and in all its later history, Athens was an almost Oriental mixture of splendid public buildings with mean and ill-grouped houses. An often-quoted saying of Demosthenes puts the matter in its most favourable light:

'The great men of old built splendid edifices for the use of the State, and set up noble works of art which later ages can never match. But in private life they were severe and simple, and the dwelling of an Aristides or a Miltiades was no more sumptuous than that of any ordinary Athenian citizen' (Third Olynthiac Oration, 25).

This is that 'desire for beauty and economy' which Pericles (or Thucydides) praised in the Funeral Oration. It has a less lovely side. Not a few passages in Greek literature speak, more or less clearly, of the streets of Athens as narrow and tortuous, unpaved, unlighted, and more like a chaos of mud and sewage than even the usual Greek road. Sparta was worse. There neither public nor private buildings were admirable, and the historian Thucydides turned aside to note the meanness of the town.

Nevertheless, the art of town-planning in Greece probably began in Athens. The architect to whom ancient writers ascribe the first step, Hippodamus of Miletus,—born about or before 480 B.C.,—seems to have worked in Athens and in connexion with Athenian cities, under the auspices of Pericles. The exact nature of his theories has not been recorded by any of the Greek writers who name him. Aristotle, however, states that he introduced the principle of straight wide streets, and that he, first of all architects, made provision for the proper grouping of dwelling-houses and also paid special heed to the combination of the different parts of a town in a harmonious whole, centred round the market-place. But there seems to be no evidence for the statement sometimes made, that he had any particular liking for either a circular or a semicircular, fan-shaped town-plan.

### *Piraeus* (fig. 2).

Three cities are named as laid out by Hippodamus. Aristotle tells us that he planned the Piraeus, the port of Athens, with broad straight streets. He does not add the precise relation of these streets to one another. If, however, the results of recent German inquiries and conjectures are correct, and if they show us his work and not—as is unfortunately very possible—the work of some later man, his design included streets running parallel or at right angles to one another and

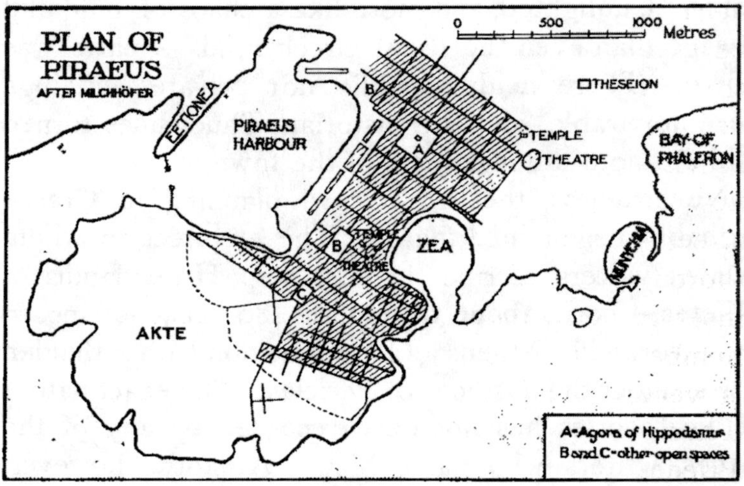


FIG. 2.

rectangular blocks of houses; the longer and presumably the more important streets ran parallel to the shore, while shorter streets ran at right angles to them down to the quays. Here is a rectangular scheme of streets, though the outline of the whole town is necessarily not rectangular (fig. 2).

## *Thurii.*

Another town ascribed to Hippodamus is the colony which the Athenians and others planted in 443 B.C. at Thurii in southern Italy, of which Herodotus himself is said to have been one of the original colonists. Its site has never been excavated, and indeed one might doubt whether excavation would show the street plan of 443 B.C. or that of a later and possibly even of a Roman age, when the town was recolonized on the Roman system. But the historian Diodorus, writing in the first century B.C. and no doubt embodying much older matter, records a pertinent detail. The town, he says, was divided lengthways by four streets and crossways by three. Plainly, therefore, it had a definite and rectangular street-planning, though the brevity of the historian does not enable us to decide how many house-blocks it had and how far the lesser streets were symmetrical with these seven principal thoroughfares. In most of the cases which we shall meet in the following sections of this treatise, the number of streets running straight or at right angles is very much greater than the number assigned to Thurii. I may refer for example to the plans of Priene, Miletus, and Timgad.

### *Rhodes.*

A third city assigned to Hippodamus is Rhodes. This, according to Strabo, was laid out by 'the architect of the Piraeus'; according to others, it was built round its harbour like the seats of an ancient theatre round the orchestra, that is, fan-fashion like Karlsruhe. However, this case is doubtful. Rhodes was laid out in 408 B.C., thirty-five years after the planting of Thurii and seventy years after the approximate date of the birth of Hippodamus. It is conceivable but not altogether probable that Hippodamus was still planning towns in his extreme old age, nor is it, on political grounds, very likely that he would be planning in Rhodes. As, however, we do not know the real date of his birth, and as Strabo does not specifically mention his name, certainty is unattainable.[1]

If we cannot tell exactly how Hippodamus planned cities or exactly which he planned, still less do we know how far town-planning on his or on any theory came into general use in his lifetime or indeed before the middle of the fourth century. Few Greek cities have been systematically uncovered, even in part. Fewer still have revealed street-planning which can be dated previous to that time. It does not follow, when we find streets in the ruins of an ancient city, that they must belong to its earliest period. That is not true of towns in any age, modern or mediaeval, Roman or Greek. Some Greek cities were founded in early times, were rebuilt in the Macedonian period, and again rebuilt in the Roman period. Without minute excava-

[1] On Hippodamus see K. F. Hermann, *de Hippodamo Milesio* (Marburg, 1841) and Erdmann, *Philologus* xlii. 193–227, and *Programm Protestant. Gymnasium zu Strassburg*, 1883. As will be seen, I do not accept all Erdmann's conclusions. For the Piraeus see Aristotle, *Politics*, II. 8 = p. 1267 and IV. 11 = p. 1330. For Thurii see Diodorus XII. 10. For Rhodes see Strabo 654=XIV. ii. 9: E. Meyer, *Gesch. des Alt.* iv. pp. 60, 199 rejects the tale. For plans of the Piraeus see Wachsmuth, *Stadt Athen im Alterthum*, ii. 134, and Curtius and Kaupert, *Karten von Attika* (1881), plan II *a* by Milchhöfer. Foucart has adduced epigraphic reasons for dating the work of Hippodamus here to 480–470 B.C. (*Journal des Savants*, 1907, pp. 178–82); they are not conclusive, but, if he be right, the difficulty of assigning the Piraeus and Rhodes to the same architect becomes even greater. The town-plan of Piraeus given by Gustav Hirschfeld (*Berichte der sächs. Ges. der Wissenschaften*, 1878, xxx. 1) is not convincing, nor do I feel very sure even about Milchhöfer's results.

tion it may be impossible to assign the town-plan of such a place to its proper place among these three periods.

We have, however, at Selinus in Sicily and Cyrene on the north coast of Africa, two cases which may belong to the age of Hippodamus. They are worth describing, since they illustrate both the difficulty of reaching quite certain conclusions and also the system which probably did obtain in the later fifth and the early fourth century.

### *Selinus* (fig. 3).

At Selinus the Italian archaeologists discovered some years ago, in the so-called Acropolis, a town of irregular, rudely pear-shaped outline with a distinct though not yet fully excavated town-plan. Two main thoroughfares ran straight from end to end and crossed at right angles (fig. 3), the longer of these thoroughfares being just a quarter of a mile long and 30 ft. wide. From these two main streets other narrower streets (12–18 ft. wide) ran off at right angles; the result, though not chess-board pattern, is a rectangular town-plan. Unfortunately, it cannot be dated. Selinus was founded in 648 B.C., was destroyed in 409, then reoccupied and rebuilt, and finally destroyed for ever in 249. Its town-planning, therefore, might be as early as the seventh century B.C. Or (and this is the most probable conclusion) it may date from the days of Selinuntine prosperity just before 409, when the city was growing and the great Temple of Zeus or Apollo was rising on its eastern hill. Or again, though less probably, it may have been introduced after 400. We may conclude that we have here a clear case of town-planning and we may best refer it to the later part of the fifth century.[1]

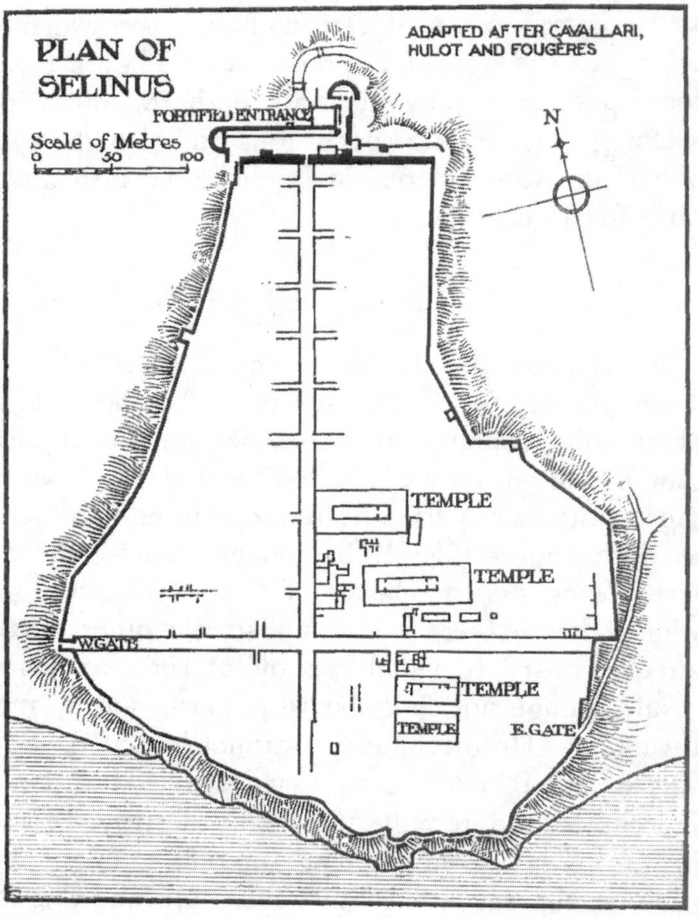


FIG. 3.

[1] Koldewey and Puchstein, *Die griech. Tempel in Unteritalien und Sicilien*, p. 90, plan 29, from Cavallari; Hulot and Fougères, *Sélinonte*, Paris, 1910, pp. 121, 168, 196. The latter writers assign the rebuilding to Hermocrates, 408–407 B.C. But our accounts of Hermocrates do not suggest that he rebuilt anything at Selinus of any sort, except defences.

*Cyrene* (fig. 4).

At Cyrene the researches of two English archaeologists about 1860 disclosed a town-plan based, like that of Selinus, on two main streets which crossed at right angles (fig. 4). Here, however, the other streets do not seem to have been planned uniformly at right angles to the two main thoroughfares, and the rectangu-

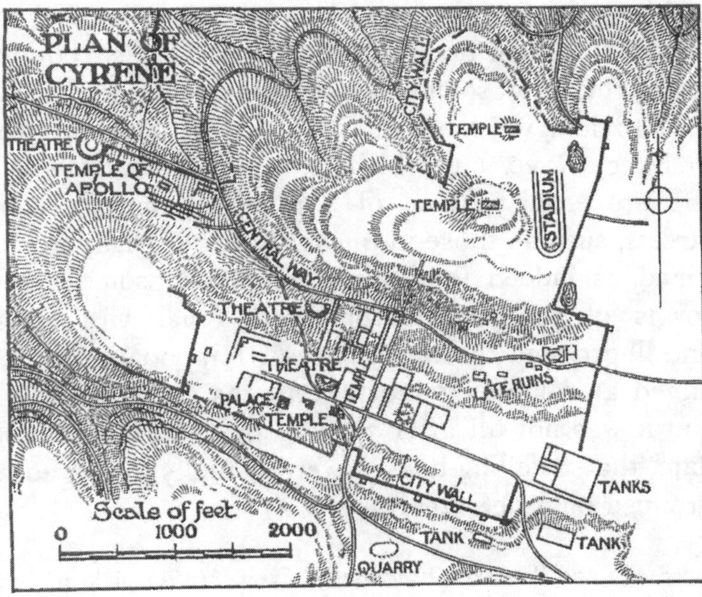


FIG. 4. (After Smith and Porcher.)

lar scheme is therefore less complete and definite than at Selinus. Cyrene, unfortunately, resembles Selinus in another respect, that we have no proper knowledge of the date when its main streets were laid out. It was founded somewhere in the seventh century B.C. and Pindar, in an ode written about 466 B.C., mentions a great processional highway there. Whether this was one of the two roads above mentioned is not clear. But it is not probable, since Pindar's road seems hardly to have been inside the city at all.[1]

In these two cases and in one or two others which might be noted from the same or later times, the town-scheme includes rectangular elements without any strict resemblance to the chess-board pattern. The dominant feature is the long straight street, of great width and splendour, which served less as the main artery of a town than as a frontage for great buildings and a route for solemn processions. Here, almost as in Babylon, we have the spectacular element which architects love, but which is, in itself, insufficient for the proper disposition of a town. Long and ample streets, such as those in question, might easily be combined, as indeed they are combined in some modern towns of southern Europe and Asia, with squalid and ill-grouped dwelling-houses. Hippodamus himself aimed at something much better, as Aristotle tells us. But it was not till after 350 B.C. or some approximate date, that dwelling-houses were actually arranged and grouped on a definite system.[2]

[1] Smith and Porcher, *Discoveries at Cyrene* (1864), plate 40 ; hence Studnickza, *Kyrene* (1890, p. 167, fig. 35), and Malten, *Kyrene* (Berlin, 1911). For Pindar's reference see Pyth. v. 90 and p. 16 above.

[2] Soluntum, near Palermo, on the north coast of Sicily, was found by Cavallari in 1875 to exhibit a rectangular street-plan ; one main street ran north and south along level ground and several lesser streets lay at right angles to it mounting a hillside by means of steps (as at Priene, p. 42). See the *Bullettino della Commissione di Antichità e Belle Arti in Sicilia*, viii. Palermo, August 1875. Cavallari himself assigned this plan to the date when Soluntum was founded—which is unfortunately uncertain—but only on the general ground that 'in una città, una volta tracciate le strade e disposte le arterie di

It was probably, however, in the first half of the fourth century that the Greek cities began to pass by-laws relating to the police, the scavenging and the general public order of their markets and streets, and to establish Agoranomi to control the markets and Astynomi to control the streets. These officials first appear in inscriptions after 350, but are mentioned

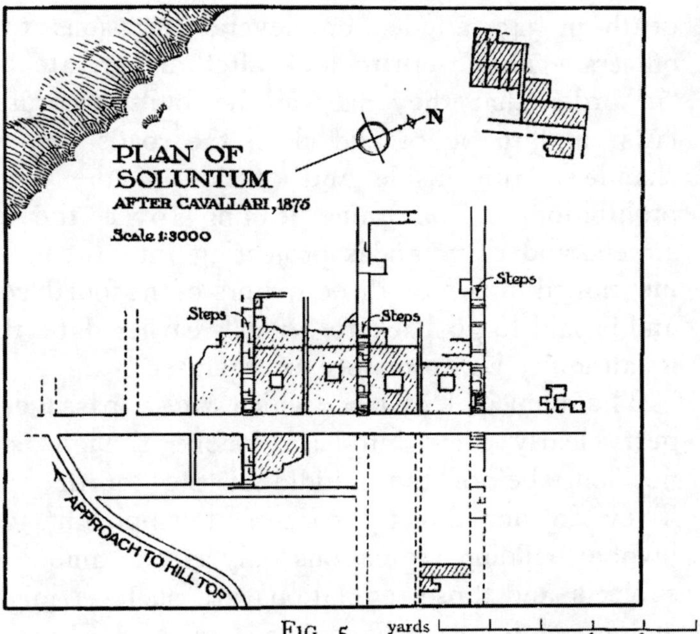


FIG. 5.

communicazione, non è facile cambiarne la disposizione generale'. I attach less weight than he does to this reason. Soluntum was in the main and by origin a Phoenician town, with a Greek colouring; in 307 B.C. it was refounded for the discharged soldiers of Agathocles; later still, in Roman times, it had the rank of 'municipium'; most of its ruins are generally considered to be of Roman date and small objects found in it are also mostly Roman, and its street-plan may also be Roman. As the 'Bulletino' is somewhat rare, I add a reduced plan (fig. 5).

in literature somewhat earlier. An account of the Athenian constitution, ascribed formerly to Xenophon and written (as is now generally agreed) about 430–424 B. C., mentions briefly the prosecution of those who built on to the public land, that is (apparently), who encroached upon the streets. But it is silent as to specific officers, Astynomi or other. Plato, however, in his 'Laws', which must date a little earlier than his death in 347, alludes on several occasions to such officers. They were to look after the private houses 'in order that they may all be built according to laws', and to police and clean the roads and water-channels, both inside and outside of the city. A prohibition of balconies leaning over the public streets, and of verandas projecting into them, is also mentioned in two or three writers of the fourth century and is said to go back to a much earlier date, though its antiquity was probably exaggerated.[1]

The municipal by-laws which these passages suggest clearly came into use before, though perhaps not long before, the middle of the fourth century. They do not directly concern town-planning; they involve building regulations only as one among many subjects, and those regulations are such as might be, and in many cases have been, adopted where town-planning was unknown. But they are natural fore-

[1] Plato, *Laws* 763 C, 779 C, &c.; Aristotle, *Ath. Pol.* 50; Arist., *Oec.* ii. 5, p. 134; Xenophon, *Ath. Pol.* iii. 4; Schol. to Aeschines, iii. 24. The fact that the word 'Astynomos' occurs in Aeschylus does not justify the writer of an article in Pauly-Wissowa (*Real-Encycl.* ii. 1870) in stating that magistrates of this title were already at work in the earlier part of the fifth century; the poet uses the noun in a general sense from which it was afterwards specialized. Some of the regulations recur at Rome (p. 137).

runners of an interest in town-planning. As in modern England, so in fourth-century Greece, their appearance suggests the growth of a care for well-ordered town life and for municipal well-being which leads directly to a more elaborate and methodical oversight of the town as an organized combination of houses and groups of houses.

As we part from this early Greek town-planning, we must admit that altogether we know little of it. There was such a thing: among its main features was a care for stately avenues: its chief architect was Hippodamus. Thus much is clear. But save in so far as Milchhöfer's plans reproduce the Piraeus of B.C. 450 or 400, we cannot discern either the shape or the size of the house-blocks, or the grouping adopted for any of the ordinary buildings, or the scheme of the ordinary roads. We may even wonder whether such things were of much account in the town-planning of that period.

# CHAPTER IV

## Greek Town-planning: the Macedonian Age, 330–130 B.C.

The Macedonian age brought with it, if not a new, at least a more systematic, method of town-planning. That was the age when Alexander and his Macedonian army conquered the East and his successors for several generations ruled over western Asia, when Macedonians and Greeks alike flocked into the newly-opened world and Graeco-Macedonian cities were planted in bewildering numbers throughout its length and breadth. Most of these cities sprang up full-grown; not seldom their first citizens were the discharged Macedonian soldiery of the armies of Alexander and his successors. The map of Turkey in Asia is full of them. They are easily recognized by their names, which were often taken from those of Alexander and his generals and successors, their wives, daughters, and relatives. Thus, one of Alexander's youngest generals, afterwards Seleucus I, sometimes styled Nicator, founded several towns called Seleucia, at least three called Apamea, and others named Laodicea and Antiochia, thereby recording himself, his Iranian wife Apama, his mother Laodice and his father Antiochus, and his successors seem to have added other towns bearing the same name. Indeed, two-thirds of the town-names which are prominent in the later history of Asia Minor and Syria, date from the age of Alexander and his Macedonians.

Many discoveries show that these towns were laid out with a regular 'chess-board' street-plan. That method of town-planning now made definite entry into the European world. No architect or statesman is recorded to have invented or systematically encouraged it. Alexander himself and his architect, one Dinocrates of Rhodes or perhaps of Macedonia, seem to have employed it at Alexandria in Egypt, and this may have set the fashion. Seven years after Alexander's death it recurs at Nicaea in Bithynia, which was refounded by one of Alexander's successors in 323 B.C. and was laid out on this fashion. But no ancient writer credits either the founder or the architect of Alexandria or the founder of Nicaea with any particular theory on the subject. If the chess-board fashion becomes now, with seeming suddenness, the common—although not the universal—rule, that is probably the outcome of the developments sketched in the last chapter. Approximations to chess-board planning had been here and there employed in the century before Alexander. When his conquests and their complicated sequel led, amongst other results, to the foundation of many new towns, it was natural that the most definite form of planning should be chosen for general use.

We might, however, wonder whether its adoption was helped by the military character of the generals who founded, and the discharged soldiers who formed the first inhabitants of so many among these towns. Military men are seldom averse to rigidity. It is worth noting, in this connexion, that when chess-board planning came into common use in the Roman Empire, many—perhaps most—of the towns to which it was applied were 'coloniae' manned by time-expired soldiers. So, too, in the Middle Ages and even in comparatively modern times, the towns laid out with rectangular street-plans in northern Italy, in Provence, in the Rhine Valley, are for the most part due in some way or other to military needs.[1] In our own days rectangular planning is a dominant feature of the largest and newest industrial towns. They are adapting a military device to the purposes of an industrial age.

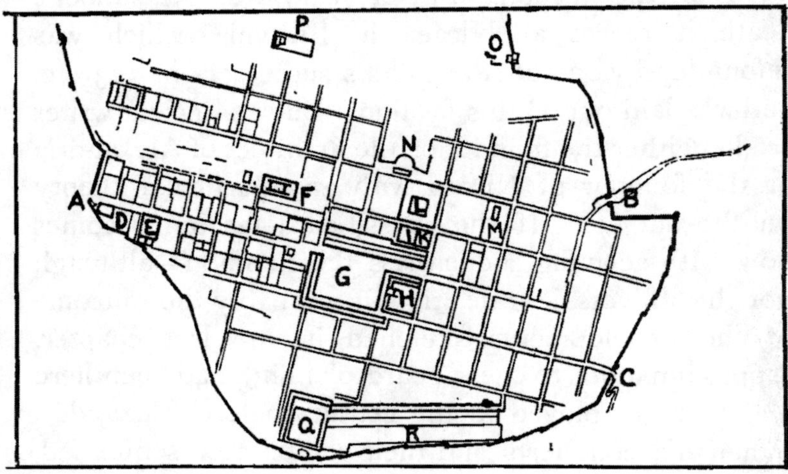


FIG. 6. GENERAL OUTLINE OF PRIENE (after Zippelius). A, B, C. Gates. D, E, F, H, M, P. Temples (see fig. 7). G. Agora, Market. I. Council House. K. Prytaneion. L, Q. Gymnasium. N. Theatre. O. Water-reservoir. R. Race-course.

[1] Since the invention of artillery, the rectangular street-plan has been regarded by soldiers as useful in defending the streets of a town. Aristotle, however, expressly observes in the *Politics* that, in street warfare, tortuous lanes were far better than straight avenues for the defence, and he recommends that the rectangular pattern should be adopted only 'in parts and in places', though he does not explain how this would work out (*Politics*, iv. 11, p. 1330).

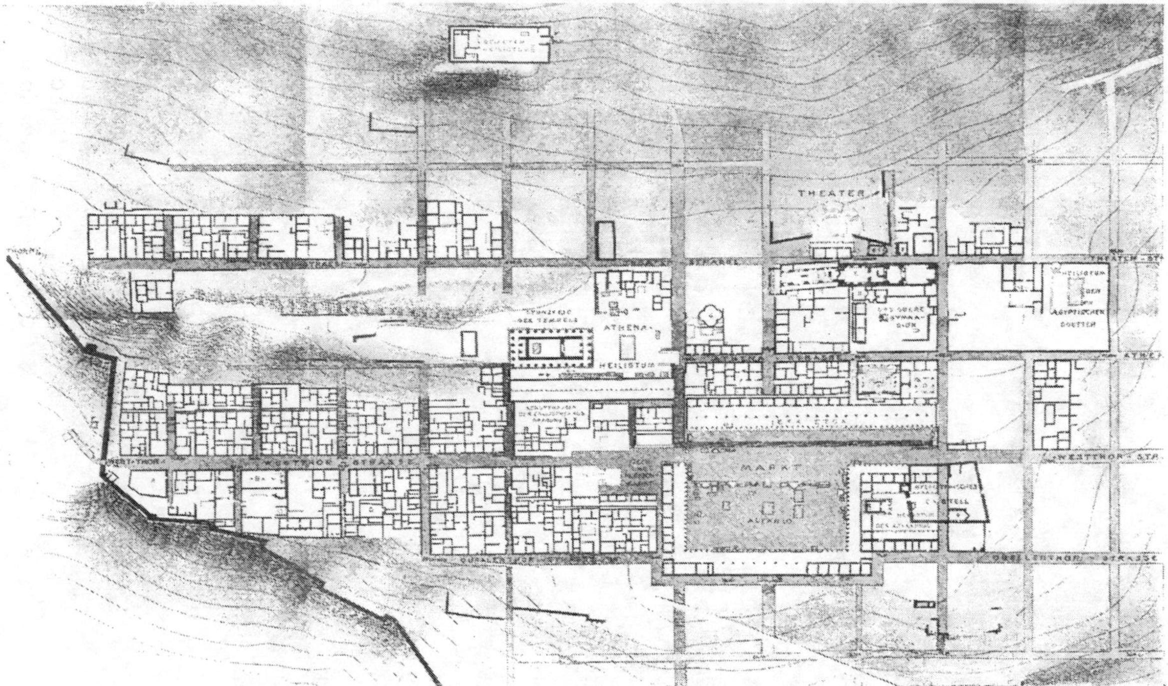


FIG. 7. PART OF PRIENE AS EXCAVATED 1895–8.
From the large plan by Wiegand and Schrader (scale : about 1:3200).

Fig. 8. Panorama of Priene, accor

From the picture by A

THE GERMAN EXCAVATIONS OF 1895–8.
us (Leipzig : Teubner).

*Priene* (figs. 6–8).

The best instance of the new system is not perhaps the most famous. Priene was a little town on the east coast of the Aegean. The high ridge of Mycale towered above it; Miletus faced it across an estuary; Samos stood out seawards to the west. In its first dim days it had been perched on a crag that juts out from the overhanging mountain; there its life began, we hardly know when, in the dawn of Greek history. But it had been worn down in the fifth century between the upper and the nether millstone of the rival powers of Samos and Miletus. Early in the Macedonian age it was refounded. The old Acropolis was given up. Instead, a broad sloping terrace, or more exactly a series of terraces, nearer the foot of the hill, was laid out with public buildings—Agora, Theatre, Stoa, Gymnasium, Temples, and so forth—and with private houses. The whole covered an area of about 750 yds. in length and 500 yds. in width. Priene was, therefore, about half the size of Pompeii (p. 63). It had, as its excavators calculate, about 400 individual dwelling-houses and a population possibly to be reckoned at 4,000.

In the centre was the Agora or market-place, with a temple and other large buildings facing on to it; round them were other public buildings and some eighty blocks of private houses, each block measuring on an average 40 × 50 yds. and containing four or five houses. The broader streets, rarely more than 23 ft. wide, ran level along the terraces and parallel to one another. Other narrower streets, generally about 10 ft. wide, ran at right angles up the slopes, with steps like those of the older Scarborough or of Assisi.[1] The whole

[1] Compare Soluntum, p. 36, n. 2.

area has not yet been explored and we do not know whether the houses were smaller or larger, richer or poorer, in one quarter than in another, but the regularity of the street-plan certainly extended over the whole site.

Despite this reasoned and systematic arrangement, no striking artistic effects appear to have been attempted. No streets give vistas of stately buildings. No squares, save that of the Agora—120 by 230 ft. within an encircling colonnade—provide open spaces where larger buildings might be grouped and properly seen. Open spaces, indeed, such as we meet, in mediaeval and Renaissance Italy or in modern English towns of eighteenth century construction, were very rare in Priene. Gardens, too, must have been almost entirely absent. In the area as yet uncovered, scarcely a single dwelling-house possessed any garden ground or yard.[1]

*Miletus* (fig. 9).

The skill of German archaeologists has revealed what town-planning meant in a small town rebuilt in the Alexandrine period. No other even approximately complete example has been as yet uncovered on any other site. But spade-work at the neighbouring and more famous city of Miletus has uncovered similar street-planning there. In one quarter, the only one yet fully excavated, the streets crossed at right angles and enclosed regular blocks of dwelling-houses measuring 32 × 60 yds. (according to the excavators) but subdivided into blocks of about 32 yds. square (fig. 9).

[1] Wiegand and Schrader, *Priene, Ergebnisse der Ausgrabung in den Jahren 1895–8* (Berlin, 1904). Professor P. Gardner gave a good account to the Town-Planning Conference (*Proceedings*, pp. 112–122). I am indebted to him for two of my illustrations.

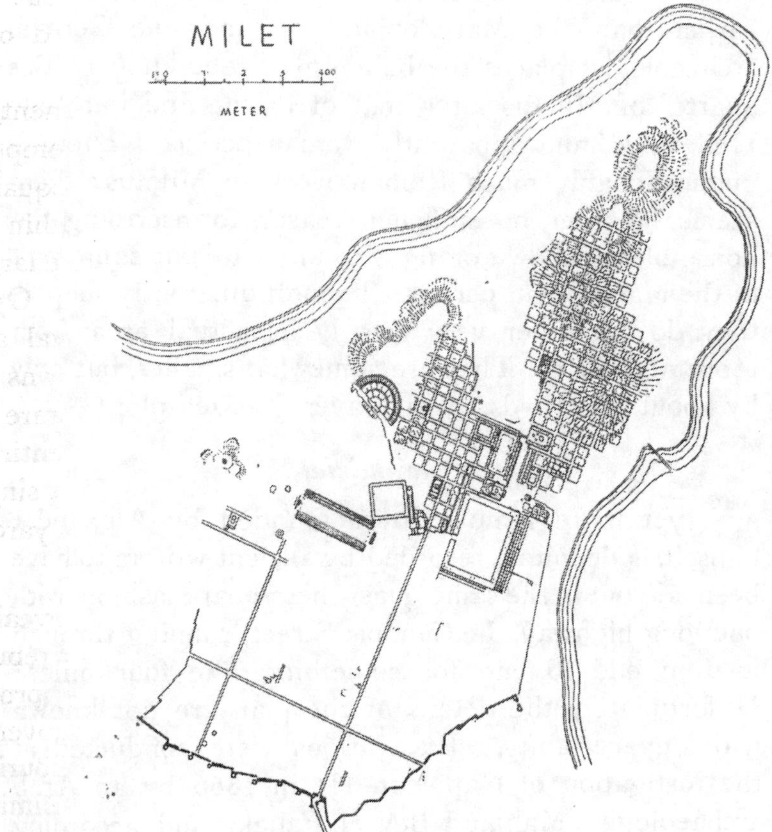


FIG. 9. MILETUS, AS EXCAVATED BY WIEGAND. (*Archäologischer Anzeiger*, 1911, p. 421.)

These blocks differ somewhat in shape from those of Priene, which are more nearly square; whether they differ in date is more doubtful. They are certainly not earlier than the Macedonian era, and one German archaeologist places the building or rebuilding of this quarter of Miletus after that of Priene and in a 'late Hellenistic' and apparently Roman period. There is unquestionably much Roman work in Miletus; there seems, however, no sufficient reason for ascribing the house-blocks shown on fig. 7 to any date but some part of the Macedonian period. Though differently shaped, they do not differ very greatly in actual area from those of Priene. They are somewhat smaller, but only by about 60 sq. yds. in each average-sized plot.[1]

### *Alexandria.*

A yet more famous town, founded by Alexander himself, is definitely recorded by ancient writers to have been laid out in the same quasi-chess-board fashion, with one long highway, the Canopic Street, running through it from end to end for something like four miles.[2] Unfortunately the details of the plan are not known with any certainty. Excavations were conducted at the instigation of Napoleon III in 1866 by an Arab archaeologist, Mahmud Bey el Fallaki, and, according to him, showed a regular and rectangular scheme in which seven streets ran east and west while thirteen ran north and south at right angles to them. The house-blocks divided by these streets were thought to vary somewhat in size but to measure in general about

[1] Wiegand, *Abhandlungen der Berliner Akademie*, 1911, Anhang; *Archäol. Anzeiger*, 1911, 420 foll.

[2] Strabo, xvii. 793.

300 × 330 metres.[1] More recent research, however, has not confirmed Mahmud's plans. The excavations of Mr. Hogarth and M. Botti suggest that many of his lines are wrong and that even his Canopic Street is incorrectly laid down. Mr. Hogarth, indeed, concludes that 'it is hopeless now to sift his work; those who would treat the site of Alexandria scientifically must ignore him and start *de novo*'. More recent excavation, carried out by Dr. Noack in 1898–9, seemed to show that the ancient streets which can now be traced beneath Alexandria belong to a Roman age, though they may of course follow older lines, and that, if some items in Mahmud's plans are possibly right, the errors and omissions are serious. We may accept as certain the statement that Alexandria was laid out with a rectangular town-plan; we cannot safely assume that Mahmud has given a faithful picture of it.[2]

### *Nicaea.*

Priene, Miletus, and Alexandria supply more or less well-known instances of Macedonian town-planning. They can be reinforced by a crowd of less famous examples, attested by literature or by actual remains. One of the most characteristic is known to us from literature, Nicaea in Bithynia, founded by one of the Macedonians in 316 B.C. and renamed by another some

[1] Mahmud Bey, *Mémoire sur l'ancienne Alexandrie* (Copenhagen, 1872); Néroutsos Bey, *L'ancienne Alexandrie* (Paris, 1888).

[2] D. G. Hogarth, *Archaeological Report of the Egypt Exploration Fund*, 1894–5, p. 28, and *Hellenic Journal*, xix. 326; F. Noack, *Athen. Mitteil.* xxv. (1900), pp. 232, 237. Dr. Noack thought that his results confirmed Mahmud; to me, as to some others, they seem rather to yield the conclusions indicated in the text.

years later in honour of his wife Nicaea. Strabo, writing about A.D. 15, describes it and his description no doubt refers to arrangements older than the Romans. It formed, he says, a perfect square in which each side measured four stades, a little over 800 yds. In each side—apparently in the middle of each side—there was one gate, and the streets within the walls were laid out at right angles to one another. A man who stood at a certain spot in the middle of the Gymnasium could see straight to all the four gates.[1] Here is the chess-board pattern in definite form, though the central portion of the city may have been laid out under the influence of spectacular effect rather than of geometry.

*Sicyon, Thebes, &c.*

Another Macedonian town-plan may be found at Sicyon, a little west of Corinth. This old Greek city was rebuilt by Demetrius Poliorcetes about 300 B.C., and is described by a Greek writer of the first century B.C. as possessing a regular plan and roads crossing at right angles. The actual remains of the site, explored in part by English and French archaeologists early in the nineteenth century, show some streets which run with mathematical straightness from north-east to south-west and others which run from north-west to south-east.[2] These streets might, indeed, date from the period when Sicyon was the chief town of the Roman province of Achaia, the period (that is) between the overthrow of Corinth in 146 B.C. and its restoration just a century later. But that was not an epoch when

[1] Strabo, 565, 566.

[2] Diodorus Sic. xx. 102; *Expédition scientifique de Morée, archit. et sculpture*, iii (1838), plate LXXXI.

such rebuilding is likely to have been carried through. Friendly as the Republican government of Rome showed itself in other ways to Hellas, there is no reason to think that it spent money on town-planning in Hellenic cities. It is far more probable that the town-plan of Sicyon dates from the Macedonians.

To the same Macedonian epoch we may perhaps ascribe the building or rather the rebuilding of Boeotian Thebes, which one who passes for a contemporary writer under the name of Dicaearchus, describes as 'recently divided up into straight streets'.[1] To the same period Strabo definitely assigns the newer town of Smyrna, lying in the plain close to the harbour. It was due, he says, to the labours of the Macedonians, Antigonus, and Lysimachus.[2] We may perhaps assign to the same period the town-planning of Mitylene in Lesbos, which Vitruvius mentions as so splendid and so unhealthy, were it not that his explanation of its unhealthiness suggests rather a fan-shaped outline than a square. It was, he says, intolerable, whatever wind might blow. With a south wind, the wind of damp and rain, every one was ill. With a north-west wind, every one coughed. With a north wind, no one could stand out of doors for the chilliness of its blasts.[3] Streets that lay open to the north and the north-west and the south, equally and alike, could only be found in a town-plan fashioned like a fan. But perhaps Vitruvius only selected three of the plagues of Lesbos.

In other cases the same planning was probably

[1] Dicaearchus, p. 143.

[2] Strabo, 646.

[3] Vitruvius, i. 6.

adopted, although the evidence as yet known shows only a rectangular plan of main streets, such as we have met in Pre-Macedonian Greece. In Macedonia itself, Thessalonika, laid out perhaps about 315 B.C., had at least one main street running southwards to the sea and two more running east and west at right angles to that.[1] In Asia two Syrian towns, which occupy sites closed to Hellenic culture before Alexander, may serve as examples. Apamea on the Orontes was built by the Macedonians, rose forthwith to importance, and retained its vigorous prosperity through the Roman Empire; in A.D. 6 it was 'numbered' by Sulpicius Quirinius, then the governor of Syria, and the census showed as many as 117,000 citizens settled in the city and its adjacent 'territory'. Its ruins seem to be mainly earlier than the Romans, and its streets may well date from its Macedonian founders. In outline it is an irregular oblong, nearly an English mile in length and varying in width from half to two-thirds of a mile. A broad and straight street, lined throughout with colonnades, runs from end to end of its length and passes at least five great buildings, which seem to be the temples and palaces of the Seleucid kings. Two other streets cross this main street at right angles. Whether the smaller thoroughfares took the same lines can be determined only by excavation. It would be a gentle guess to think so.[2]

Further south, on the edge of the Hauran, stood the town of Gerasa. This too, like Apamea, was built by

[1] Tafrali, *Topographie de Thess.* pp. 121 foll. and plan.

[2] E. Sachau, *Reise in Syrien* (1883), p. 76; Mommsen, *Ephemeris epigr.* iv, p. 514, and *Mon. Ancyr.* (ed. 2), p. 540.

the Macedonians and flourished not only in their days but during the following Roman age. Its general outline was ovoid, its greatest diameter three quarters of a mile, its area some 235 acres—nearly the same with Roman Cologne and Roman Cirencester. Its streets resembled those of Apamea. A colonnaded highway

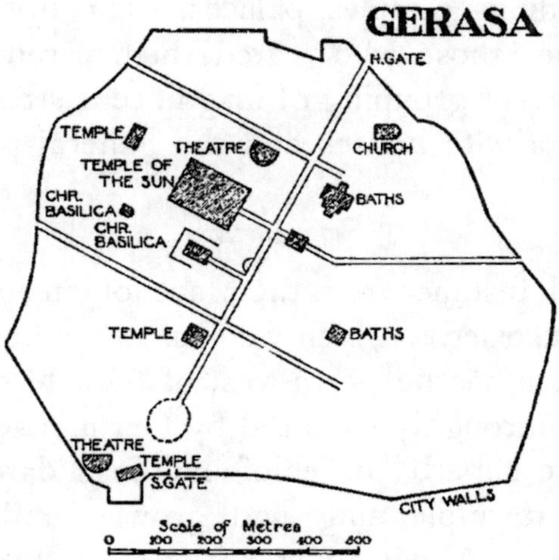


FIG. 10. (After G. Schumacher.)

ran straight through from north to south; two other streets crossed at right angles, and its chief public buildings, the Temple of the Sun and three other temples, two theatres and two public baths, stood near these three streets (fig. 10). Again the evidence proves rectangular town-planning in broad outline; excavation alone can tell the rest.[1]

In the towns just described a distinctive feature is

[1] *Zeitschrift des deutschen Palästina-Vereins*, xxv (1902), plate 6; Bädeker, *Palestine and Syria* (1906), p. 140. For the neighbouring Bostra, see p. 136.

the 'chess-board' pattern of streets and rectangular house-blocks. That, of course, is the feature which most concerns us here. It may not have looked so predominant to their builders and inhabitants. The towns which the Macedonians founded were not seldom rich and large; several were the capitals of powerful and despotic rulers. In such towns we expect great public buildings, temples, palaces. It is not surprising if sometimes those who reared them cared solely for the spectacular grouping of magnificent structures and forgot the private houses and the general plan of the town.

*Pergamum.*

One such instance from the Macedonian age, perhaps the most instructive which we could ever hope to get,[1] is Pergamum, in the north-west of Asia Minor. This has been thoroughly explored by German science; its remains are superb; its chief buildings date from an age when town-planning had grown familiar to the Greek world. About 300 B.C. it was a hill-town where a Macedonian chief could bestow a war-chest. It grew both populous and splendid in the third and second centuries B.C. under the Attalid kings; later builders, Augustus or Trajan or other, added little either to its general design or to its architectural glory. The dominant idea was that of a semi-circle of great edifices, crowning the crest and inner slopes of a high crescent-shaped ridge. Near the northern and highest end of this ridge stood the palace of the Attalid princes,

[1] Ephesus, refounded by Lysimachus about 281 B.C., might perhaps be another. But the repeated excavations there, though they have taught us much about the temples and other large edifices of the great city, seem to have left the streets comparatively unexplored.

afterwards buried beneath a temple in honour of Trajan. Next, to the south, was the Library—with stores of papyri worth more perhaps to the world than all the architecture of Pergamon. The middle of the crescent held the shrine of Athena, goddess of Pergamon, and beside it the Altar of Zeus the Saviour, gigantic in size, splendid with sculpture, itself the equal of an Acropolis. Lastly, the southern or lower end of the ridge bore a temple of Dionysus and an Agora for Assemblies.

These buildings ringed the hill-top in stately semicircle; below them, a theatre was hewn out of the slopes and a terrace 250 yds. long was held up by buttresses against precipitous cliffs. Lower yet, beneath the Agora, the town of common men covered the lower hill-side in such order or disorder as its steepness allowed. Here was no conventional town-planning. Only a yet lower and later city, built in Roman days on more or less level spaces beside the stream Selinus, seems perhaps to have been laid out in chess-board fashion.[1] The Attalid kings, the founders of Pergamon, cared only for splendid buildings splendidly adorned. If their abrupt hill-side forbade the straight and broad processional avenues of some other Greek cities, they crowned their summits instead with a crescent of temples and palaces which had not its like on the shores of the Aegean.

Yet even Pergamon had its building-laws and by-laws for the protection of common life. A Pergamene inscription contains part of a 'Royal Law' which

[1] P. Schatzmann, *Athen. Mitteil.* xxxv. (1910) 385; *Archäol. Anzeiger* (1910), p. 541. This lowest city is covered by a swarm of modern houses and hovels, and has not been very fully explored.

apparently dates from one of the Attalid rulers. It is imperfect. But we can recognize some of the items for which it provided. Houses which fell or threatened to fall on to the public street, or which otherwise became ruinous, could be dealt with by the Astynomi; if their owners failed to repair them, these magistrates were to make good the defects themselves and to recover the cost, and a fine over and above it, from the owners; if the Astynomi neglected their duty, the higher magistrates, the Strategi, were to take up the matter. Streets were to be cleaned and scavenged by the same Astynomi. Brick-fields were expressly forbidden within the city. The widths of roads outside the town were fixed and owners of adjacent land were held liable for their repair, and there was possibly some similar rule, not preserved on the inscription, for roads inside the walls; at Priene, it seems, these latter were in the care of the municipality. There were provisions, too, for the repair of common walls which divided houses belonging to two owners, and also for the prevention of damp where two houses stood side by side on a slope and the wall of the lower house stood against the soil beneath the upper house.[1]

These rules are very like those which were coming into use before 330 B.C. (p. 37). Only, they are more elaborate, and it is significant that the inscriptions begin in Macedonian and later days to give more and fuller details as to the character of these laws and as to the existence in many cities of officials to execute them. It is not surprising to find that Roman legislation of the time of Caesar and the early Empire applies these

[1] Kolbe, *Athen. Mitteil.* xxvii. 47 and xxix. 75; Hitzig, *Zeitschrift der Savigny-Stiftung, roman. Abteilung* xxvi. 433.

or very similar rules to the local government of the Roman municipalities of the Empire (p. 137).

So common in the Macedonian world was the town-planning which has been described above, that the literature of the period, even in its casual phrases and incidental similes, speaks of towns as being normally planned in this fashion. Two examples from two very different authors will suffice as illustration. Polybius, writing somewhere about B.C. 150, described in well-known chapters the scheme of the Roman camp, and he concludes much as follows: 'This being so, the whole outline of the camp may be summed up as right-angled and four-sided and equal-sided, while the details of its street-planning and its general arrangement are precisely parallel to those of a city' (VI. 31, 10). He was comparing the Greek town, as he knew it in his own country, with the encampment of the Roman army; he found in the town the aptest and simplest parallel which he could put before his readers. A much later writer, living in a very different environment and concerned with a very different subject, fell nevertheless under the influence of the same ideas. Despite his 'sombre scorn' for things Greek and Roman, St. John, when he wished to figure the Holy City Jerusalem, centre of the New Heaven and New Earth, pictured it as a city lying foursquare, the length as large as the breadth, and entered by twelve gates, 'on the east three gates, on the north three gates, on the south three gates, and on the west three gates.'[1]

[1] Revelation xxi. 13, 16. Some of the details are, no doubt, drawn from the later chapters of Ezekiel, but the difference between the two writers is plain.

The instances and items cited in the preceding paragraphs lie within the limits of the Greek world and of the Roman Empire. We might perhaps wish to pursue our speculations and ask whether this vigorous system influenced foreign lands, and whether the Macedonian army carried the town-plan of their age, in more or less perfect form, as far as their conquests reached. Alexander settled many soldiers in lands which were to form his eastern and north-eastern frontiers, as if against the central-asiatic nomads. Merv and Herat, Khokand and Kandahar,[1] have been thought—and, it seems, thought with some reason—to date from the Macedonian age and in their first period to have borne the name Alexandria. But no Aurel Stein has as yet uncovered their ruins, and speculation about them is mere speculation.

[1] See p. 145 below.

# CHAPTER V

## Italian Town-planning. The Origins

If Greek and Macedonian town-planning are fairly well known, the Roman Empire offers a yet larger mass of certain facts, both in Italy and in the provinces. The beginnings, naturally, are veiled in obscurity. We can trace the system in full work at the outset of the Empire; we cannot trace the steps by which it grew. Evidences of something that resembles town-planning on a rectangular scheme can be noted in two or three corners of early Italian history—first in the prehistoric Bronze Age, then in a very much later Etruscan town, and thirdly on one or two sites of middle Italy connected with the third or fourth century B.C. These evidences are scanty and in part uncertain, and their bearing on our problem is not always clear, but they claim a place in an account of Italian town-planning. To them must be added, fourthly, the important evidence which points to the use of a system closely akin to town-planning in early Rome itself.

### *The Terremare* (fig. 11).

(i) We begin in the Bronze Age, somewhere between 1400 and 800 B.C., amidst the so-called Terremare. More than a hundred of these strange settlements have been examined by Pigorini, Chierici, and other competent Italians. Most of them occur in a well-defined district between the Po and the Apennines, with Piacenza at its west end and Bologna at its east end. Some have also been noted on the north bank of the Po near Mantua, both east and west of the Mincio, and two or three elsewhere in Italy. Archaeologically, they all belong to the Bronze Age; they seem, further, to be the work of a race distinct from any previous dwellers in North Italy, which had probably just moved south from the Danubian plains. At some time or other this race had dwelt in lake-villages. They were now settled on dry ground and far away from lakes—one of their hamlets is high in the Apennines, nearly 1,900 ft. above the sea. But they still kept in the Terremare the lacustrine fashion of their former homes.

The nature of these strange villages can best be explained by an account of the best-known and the largest example of them (fig. 11). At Castellazzo di Fontanellato, a little west of Parma, are the vestiges of a settlement which, with its defences, covered an area of about forty-three acres. In outline it was four-sided; its east and west sides were parallel to one another, and the whole resembled a rectangle which had been pulled a trifle askew. Round it ran a solid earthen rampart, 50 ft. broad at the base and strengthened with woodwork (plan, B). In front of the rampart was a wet ditch (A), 100 ft. wide, fed with fresh water from a neighbouring brook by an inlet at the south-western corner (C) and emptied by an outfall on the east (D). One wooden bridge gave access to this artificial island at its southern end (E). The area within the rampart, a little less than thirty acres in extent, was divided into four parts by two main streets, which would have intersected at right angles had the place been strictly rectangular; other narrower streets ran parallel to these main thoroughfares. On the east side (F) was a small 'citadel'—*arx* or *templum*—with ditch, rampart and bridge of its own (G, H); in this were a trench and some pits (K) which seemed by their contents to be connected with ritual and religion. Outside the whole

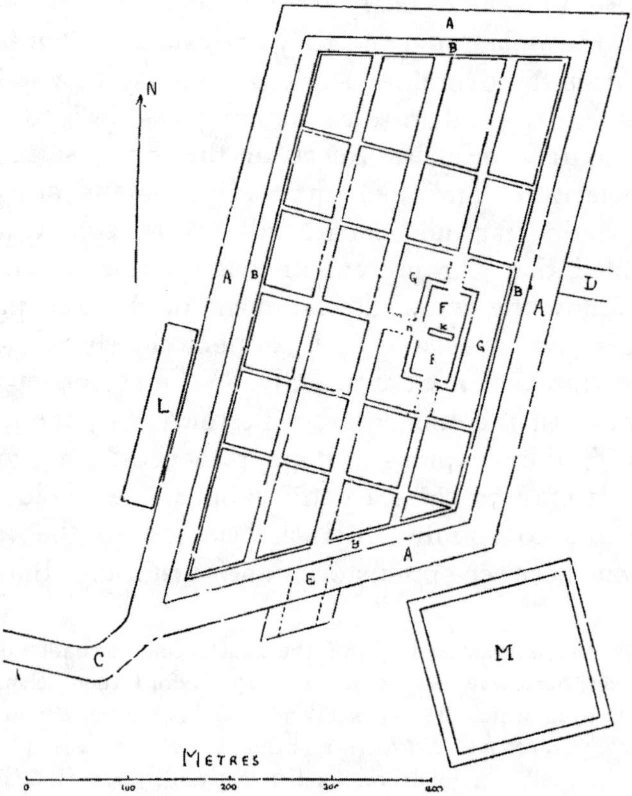


FIG. 11. TERRAMARA OF CASTELLAZZO DI FONTANELLATO.

(L, M) were two cemeteries, platforms of urns set curiously like the village itself, and also a little burning *ghat*.[1] The population of the village is necessarily

[1] The literature of the Terremare is very large. The results obtained up to 1894 were summarized by F. von Duhn in the *Neue*

doubtful. A German writer, Nissen, has reckoned it at four or five thousand, men, women and children together, crowded into small huts. But this estimate may be too high. In any case, many of the Terremare are much smaller.

These Terremare bear a strong likeness to the later Italian town-planning, and they are usually taken to be the oldest discoverable traces of that system. This means that the Italian town-planning was derived from other sources besides Greece or the East, since the Terremare are far older than Hippodamus or even Nebuchadnezzar and Sennacherib (pp. 23, 29). It must be added that our present knowledge does not allow us to follow the actual development of the Terremare into historic times, and to link them closely with the later civilization of Central Italy. When some modern scholars call the men of the Terremare by the name 'Italici', they express a hope rather than a proven fact. It may be safer, for the moment, to avoid that name and to refrain from theories as to the exact relation between prehistoric and historic. But we

*Heidelberger Jahrbücher*, iv. 144; the best recent accounts are by T. E. Peet, *Stone and Bronze Ages in Italy* (Oxford, 1909), chaps. 14 and 17, from which fig. 11 is taken, and R. Munro, *Palaeolithic Man and Terramara Settlements* (Edin., 1912), pp. 291–487 and plates xxxiii foll. A good brief sketch is given by Mr. H. S. Jones, *Companion to Roman History*, pp. 4–6. One point in the arrangement seems not quite clear. It is generally stated that the trapezoidal outline was adopted in order to allow the water to enter the ditch from a running stream and to part easily into two channels (fig. 11). That is quite intelligible. But, if so, one would expect the outlet to be at the opposite end, and not (as it actually is) in the middle of one side, where it would 'short-circuit' the current. (Mr. H. S. Jones seems to have confused inlet and outlet.)

shall see below that the existence of a relation between the two is highly probable.

*Marzabotto* (fig. 12).

(ii) A greater puzzle, dating probably from the fifth century B.C., meets us in the ruins of a nameless little Etruscan town which stood outside of Etruria

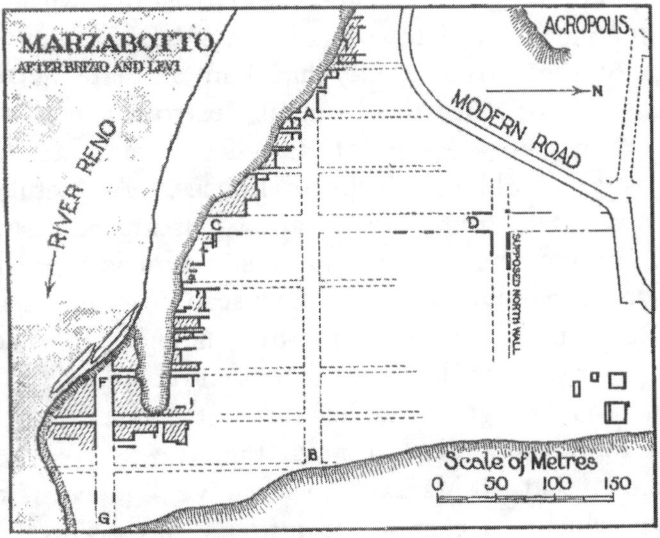


FIG. 12.
(AB, FG, CD, main streets. The shading represents excavated houses.)

proper, on the north slopes of the Apennines. Its site is fifteen miles south of Bologna, close to the modern Marzabotto, on the left bank of the little river Reno. Only a tiny part has been uncovered. But the excavators have not hesitated to complete their results conjecturally into a rectangular town-plan, with streets crossing at right angles and oblong blocks of houses measuring from 158 to 176 yds. in length and 37 or 44 or 71 yds. in width (fig. 12). The whole must have been laid out at once, and the smaller remains seem to show that this was done by Etruscans. In the fourth century the place was sacked by the Gauls, and though there was later occupation,[1] its extent is doubtful.[2]

Further excavation is, however, needed to confirm this generally accepted interpretation of the place. Nothing has been noted elsewhere in Etruria or its confines to connect the Etruscans with any rectangular form of town-plan. At Veii, for example, most of the Etruscan city has lain desolate and unoccupied ever since the Romans destroyed it, but the site shows no vestige of streets crossing at right angles or of oblong blocks of houses. At Vetulonia the excavated fragment of an Etruscan city shows only curving and irregular streets.[3] Nor is there real reason to believe that the 'Etruscan teaching' learnt by Rome included an art of town-planning (p. 71) or that, as a recent French writer has conjectured, the Etruscans brought any such art with them from the East and communicated it to the West. We must conclude that at Marzabotto we have a piece of evidence which we cannot set into its proper historical framework. We might perhaps call it an early blend of Greek and Italian methods and compare it with Naples (p. 100). It is odd that four out of seven house-blocks should measure just under 120 Roman ft. in width and thus approximate to a figure which

[1] *Archaeological Journal*, 1903, p. 237.

[2] Brizio, *Monumenti Antichi*, i. 252, superseding Gozzadini's *Antica Necropoli a Marzabotto* (Bologna, 1865–70); Grenier, *Bologne villanovienne* &c. (Paris, 1912) p. 98. Compare *Authority and Archaeology*, pp. 305, 306.

[3] *Notizie degli Scavi* 1895, p. 272; Durm, *Baukunst der Etr.* p. 39.

we meet often elsewhere in the Roman world (p. 79). But it would be well to learn more of the plan by further excavation.

### *Pompeii* (fig. 13).

(iii) A third piece of evidence can be found on a site which historians and novelists alike connect mainly with the Roman Empire, but which dates back to the days of the early or middle Republic. Pompeii began in or before the sixth century B.C. as an Oscan city. For a while, we hardly know when, it was ruled by Etruscans. Later, about 420 B.C., it was occupied by Samnites. Finally, it became Roman; it was refounded in 80 B.C. as a 'colonia' and repeopled by soldiers discharged from the armies of Sulla. In A.D. 79 it reached its end in the disaster to which it owes its fame. Its life, therefore, was long and full of destruction, re-building, enlargement. Its architectural history is naturally hard to follow. Many of its buildings, however, can be dated more or less roughly by the style of their ornament or the character of their material, and the lines of its streets suggest some conjectures as to its growth which deserve to be stated even though they may conflict with the received opinions about Pompeii. It will be understood, of course, that these conjectures, like all speculations on Pompeii, are limited by the fact that barely half of its area has been as yet uncovered, and that very little search has been made beneath the floors and pavements of its latest period.[1]

[1] For recent plans of Pompeii the reader may consult the second edition (1908) of August Mau's *Pompeii*, or the fifth edition (1910) of his *Führer durch Pompeii*, re-edited by W. Barthel. A plan on a large

As we know it at present, Pompeii is an irregular oval area of about 160 acres, planted on a small natural hill and girt with a stone wall nearly two miles in circumference (fig. 13). On the west there was originally access to the sea, and on this side the walls have disappeared or have not been yet uncovered. Near this end of the town is the Forum, with the principal temples and public buildings round it. At the east

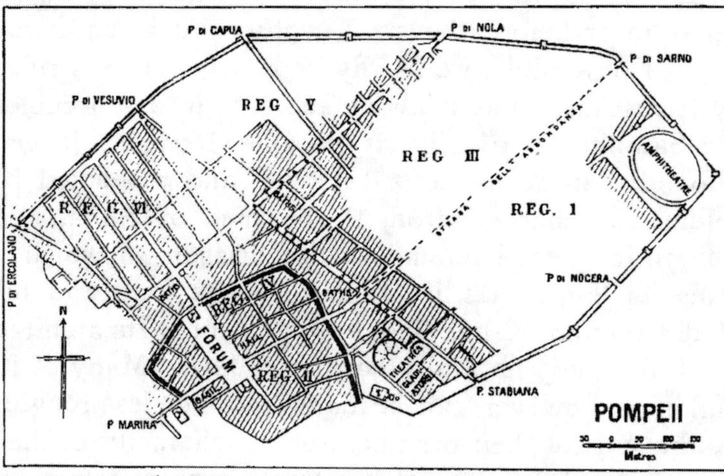


FIG. 13. (T = Temple. The area of the supposed original settlement is outlined in black.)

end of the town, nearly 1200 yds. from the western extremity, is the amphitheatre, and the town-walls appear to have been drawn so as to include it. Two main streets, now called the Strada di Nola and the Strada dell' Abbondanza, cross the town from SW. to NE. The main streets from NW. to SE. are less distinct, but the Strada Stabiana certainly ran from wall to wall. While there is some appearance of

scale is given in the last part of *CIL.* iv (1909); there are also occasional plans in the *Notizie degli Scavi*. See also C. Weichardt, *Pompeji vor der Zerstörung* (Leipzig, 1897).

symmetry in the streets generally, it does not go very far ; there is hardly a right angle, or any close approach to a right angle, at any street corner.

It is generally held, as Mau has argued, that the whole town was laid out at once, perhaps during the Etruscan period, on one plan of streets crossing at right angles. Two principal streets, those now styled the Strada di Mercurio and the Strada di Nola, are considered to be the main streets of this earliest town-plan, and to give it its general direction. A third main street, the Strada Stabiana, which cuts obliquely across from the Vesuvian to the Stabian Gate and mars the supposed symmetry of this town-plan, is ascribed to the influence of a small natural depression along which it runs, while a small area east of the Forum, which also breaks loose from the general scheme, is thought to have been laid out abnormally in order to remedy the effect of this obliquity.[1]

This theory is open to objections. In the first place the streets (even apart from those just east of the Forum) do not really form one symmetrical plan. Region VI fits very ill with Regions I and III. Both indicate systematic planning. But Region VI is laid out in oblong blocks 110 ft. wide and either 310 ft. or 480 ft. long, while Regions I and III are made up of approximately square blocks about 200 ft. each way. Moreover, the orientation of the blocks is different. Those in Region VI follow the lines of the Strada di Mercurio; those of Regions I and II, and perhaps also of Region V, are dominated by the Strada Stabiana. Yet there is no obvious reason why this difference

[1] Mau, *Führer* (1910), p. 5, 'um die Schiefwinkeligkeit zu vermindern.' Truly, a very inadequate reason.

should not have been avoided; it results, indeed, in awkward corners and inconvenient spaces. Nor, again, can we accept as in any degree adequate the cause assigned by Mau for the odd orientation of the streets next to the east side of the Forum.

These streets which lie round and east of the Forum suggest a different development. Pompeii may have begun with a little Oscan town planted in what became its south-western corner, near the Water-Gate and the Forum, within the area of Regions II and IV. Here is a little network of streets, about 300 by 400 yds. across (25 acres), which harmonizes ill with the streets in the rest of the town, which lies close to the river-haven on the Sarno, which includes the Forum and Basilica—probably the oldest public sites, though not the oldest surviving structures, in Pompeii—and which is large enough to have formed the greater part or even the whole of a prehistoric city. The earliest building as yet excavated at Pompeii, the Doric Temple, with its precinct now known as the Forum Triangulare, stood on the edge of this area looking out from its high cliff over the plain of the Sarno. Originally this Temple may have stood just within the first town-wall, or perhaps just without it, sheltered by the precipice which it crowns. This area has all the appearance of an 'Altstadt'. No doubt it has been much altered by later changes. In particular, Forum and Basilica have grown far beyond their first proportions, and the buildings which surround them have been added, altered, enlarged out of all resemblance to the original plan. Nevertheless, this theory seems to account better than any other for this curious little corner of streets that are hardly regular even in their relations to one another and are wholly irreconcilable to the rest of the town.

Round this primitive city grew up the greater Pompeii. The growth must have been rather by two or three distinct accretions than a gradual and continuous development. At present we cannot trace these stages. To do that we must wait till the excavations can be carried deeper down, and till the other half of the city has been uncovered, or at least till the lines of its streets and the shapes of its house-blocks have been determined, like those of Priene (p. 42), by special inquiry. All that is as yet certain is that Regions I, III, V, and VI were laid out, and their houses were (in part at least) in existence before—perhaps long before—80 B.C., when the Sullan colony was planted,[1] and we see also that Region VI is planned differently from I and III.

Another fact claims notice. The town-planning of Pompeii is in the main trapezoidal, not rectangular. Neither its oblongs, nor its squares, nor its street-crossings exhibit true right angles, though many of the rooms and peristyles in the private houses are regular enough. In this feature Pompeii resembles the trapezoidal outlines of the Terremare (fig. 11). It resembles also much Roman military work, both of Republican and of Imperial date, which disregards the strict right angle and accepts squares and oblongs which are, so to say, askew. The motive of the Terremare is supposed to have been, as I have said above, that of providing an easy flow for the water in the encircling moat. The motive of various military

[1] Region VI contains an ancient column of the sixth century B.C. (Mau, *Führer*, p. 113), but this may not be *in situ*.

camps may perhaps be found rather in a wish to secure the same area as that of an orthodox rectangle, even though the ground forbade the strict execution of the orthodox figure. Whatever the reason, the trapezoidal house-blocks of Pompeii exhibit a feature which is not alien to the earlier town-planning of Italy, though it is strange to the cities of Greece.

### *Norba.*

Not only do we need to know more of Pompeii itself. We need evidence also from other Italian towns of similar age. Here our ignorance is deep. Only one site which can help has been even tentatively explored. Norba, which once crowned a spur of the Monti Lepini above the Pontine marshes, was founded as a Roman town, according to the orthodox chronology, in 492 B.C.[1] But the received chronology of the earlier Republic, minute as it looks, probably deserves no more credence than the equally minute but mainly fictitious dates assigned by the Saxon Chronicle to the beginnings of English History. Actual remains found at Norba suggest rather that it was founded (not necessarily by Rome) about, or a little before, 300 B.C.; it is therefore later than the Terremare and Marzabotto, and later also than the Oscan age of Pompeii. On the other hand, it came to an end in the Sullan period (82 B.C.). Its excavation has little more than begun, but it already indicates a scheme of streets somewhat resembling that of Pompeii,[2] and it is a useful adjunct to our better knowledge of

[1] Livy ii. 34, contradicted, however, by xxvii. 10 and by Dionysius Halic. vii. 13 *ad fin.*

[2] *Notizie degli Scavi,* 191, p. 558, 1903, p. 261; Frothingham,

the more famous town. The two together furnish examples of the town-planning of middle Italy of about 400–300 B.C., in days that are only half historic, and thus help to fill the gap between the Terremare and the fully developed system of the Roman Imperial period.

It may be permitted in this context to add a plan of a north Italian city, in which some of the modern streets recall one quarter of Pompeii (fig. 14). Modena, the Roman Mutina, was founded as a 'colonia' with 2,000 male settlers in 183 B.C., and despite various misfortunes became one of the chief towns in the Lombard plain. One part of this town shows a row of long narrow blocks measuring about 20 × 160 metres (fig. 14, plan A), with a second row of shorter blocks of the same width and about half the length (plan B). These blocks have been much marred and curtailed by the inevitable changes of town life, but their symmetry cannot be accidental, and if they date back, as is quite possible, to Roman days, they may be put beside the Sixth Region of Pompeii which contains two rows of similar blocks.[1]

(iv) There remains, fourthly, evidence relating to early Rome itself, and to customs and observances which obtained there. These customs belong to the

*Roman Cities*, plate ix. I am indebted to Dr. T. Ashby, Director of the British School at Rome, for information as to the site. Excavations made in 1823 at the Roman Falerii (founded 241 B.C.) show streets crossing at right angles, but the piece unearthed was small and the date uncertain (Canina, *Etruria Maritima* i, plate ix).

[1] Fig. 14 is taken from Zuccagni-Orlandini (1844). Kornemann suggests that Mutina was refounded about 40–20 B.C., but there seems to be no evidence of this break in its continuity.

three fields of religion, agrarian land-settlement and war. All three exhibit the same principle, the division of a definite space by two straight lines crossing at right angles at its centre, and (if need be) the further division of such space by other lines parallel to the

**MODENA**

FIG. 14. See p. 69.

two main lines. The Roman augur who asked the will of Heaven marked off a square piece of sky or earth—his *templum*—into four quarters ; in them he sought for his signs. The Roman general who encamped his troops, laid out their tents on a rectangular pattern governed by the same idea. The commissioners who assigned farming-plots on the public domains to emigrant citizens of Rome, planned these plots on the same rectangular scheme—as the map of rural Italy is witness to this day.

These Roman customs are very ancient. Later Romans deemed them as ancient as Rome itself, and, though such patriotic traditions belong rather to politics than to history, we find the actual customs well established when our knowledge first becomes full, about 200 B.C.[1] The Roman camp, for example, had reached its complex form long before the middle of the second century, when Polybius described it in words. Here, one can hardly doubt, are things older even than Rome. Scholars have talked, indeed, of a Greek origin or of an Etruscan origin, and the technical term for the Roman surveying instrument, *groma*, has been explained as the Greek word 'gnomon', borrowed through an Etruscan medium. But the name of a single instrument would not carry with it the origin of a whole art, even if this etymology were more certain than it actually is. Save for the riddle of Marzabotto (p. 61), we have no reason to connect the Etruscans with town-planning or with the Roman system of surveying. When the Roman antiquary Varro alleged that 'the Romans founded towns with Etruscan ritual', he set the fashion for many later assertions by Roman and modern writers.[2] But he did not prove his allegation, and it is not

[1] The prologue to the Poenulus of Plautus (verse 49) which mentions 'limites' and a 'finitor', may well be as old as Plautus himself. But the 'centuriation' still visible in north Italy around colonies planted about 180 B.C. is no full proof of rectangular surveying at that date. These towns were re-founded at a much later date, and their lands, and even their streets, *may* have been laid out anew.

[2] Varro *ling. lat.* 5. 143 *oppida condebant Etrusco ritu, id est, iunctis bobus*, cf. Frontinus *de limit.* (grom. i. p. 27).

so clear as is generally assumed, that he meant 'Etruscan ritual' to include architectural town-planning as well as religious ceremonial.

These are Italian customs, far older than the beginnings of Greek influence on Rome, older than the systematic town-planning of the Greek lands, and older also than the Etruscans. They should be treated as an ancestral heritage of the Italian tribes kindred with Rome, and should be connected with the plan of Pompeii and with the far older Terremare. Many generations in the family tree have no doubt been lost. The genealogy can only be taken as conjectural. But it is a reasonable conjecture.

In their original character these customs were probably secular rather than religious. They took their rise as methods proved by primitive practice to be good methods for laying out land for farming or for encamping armies. But in early communities all customs that touched the State were quasi-religious; to ensure their due performance, they were carried out by religious officials. At Rome, therefore, more especially in early times, the augurs were concerned with the delimitation alike of farm-plots and of soldiers' tents. They testified that the settlement, whether rural or military, was duly made according to the ancestral customs sanctioned by the gods. After-ages secularized once more, and as they secularized, they also introduced science. It was, perhaps, Greek influence which brought in a stricter use of the rectangle and a greater care for regular planning.

It may be asked how all this applies to the planning of towns. We possess certainly no such clear evidence with respect to towns as with respect to divisions agrarian or military. But the town-plans which we shall meet in the following chapters show very much the same outlines as those of the camp or of the farm plots. They are based on the same essential element of two straight lines crossing at right angles in the centre of a (usually) square or oblong plot. This is an element which does not occur, at least in quite the same form, at Priene or in other Greek towns of which we know the plans, and it may well be called Italian. We need not hesitate to put town and camp side by side, and to accept the statement that the Roman camp was a city in arms. Nor need we hesitate to conjecture further that in the planning of the town, as in that of the camp, Greek influence may have added a more rigid use of rectangular 'insulae'. When that occurred, will be discussed in Chapter VI.

Whether the nomenclature of the augur, the soldier and the land-commissioner was adopted in the towns, is a more difficult, but fortunately a less important question. Modern writers speak of the *cardo* and the *decumanus* of Roman towns, and even apply to them more highly technical terms such as *striga* and *scamnum*. For the use of *cardo* in relation to towns there is some evidence (p. 107). But it is very slight, and for the use of the other terms there is next to no evidence at all.[1] The silence alike of literature and of inscriptions shows that they were, at the best,

[1] Whether the *possessores ex vico Lucretio scamno primo* of Cologne (Corpus XIII. 8254) had their property inside the 'colonia' of that place or in the country outside, may be doubted (Schulten, *Bonner Jahrb.* ciii. 28).

theoretical expressions, confined to the surveyor's office.[1]

[1] The phrase Roma Quadrata ought, perhaps, to be mentioned in this chapter. It does not seem, however, to be demonstrably older than the Ciceronian age. The line *et qui sextus erat Romae regnare quadratae*, once attributed to Ennius (ed. Vahlen, 1854, 158), is clearly of much later date. As a piece of historical evidence, the phrase merely sums up some archaeologist's theory (very likely a correct theory, but still a theory) that the earliest Rome on the Palatine had a more or less rectangular outline.

# CHAPTER VI

## Italian Town-planning: the Late Republic and Early Empire

During the later Republic and the earlier Empire many Italian towns were founded or re-founded. To this result several causes contributed. Like the Greeks before them, the Romans of the Republic sent out from time to time compact bodies of emigrants whenever the home population had grown too large for its narrow space. These bodies were each large enough to form a small town, and thus each migration meant—or might mean—the foundation of a new town full-grown from its birth. The Greeks generally established new and politically independent towns. The Romans followed another method. Their colonists remained subject to Rome and constituted new centres of Roman rule, small quasi-fortresses of Roman dominion in outlying lands. Often the military need for such a stronghold had more to do with the foundation of a 'colonia' than the presence of too many mouths in the city. Cicero, speaking of a 'colonia' planted at Narbo (now Narbonne) in southern Gaul about 118 B.C., and planted perhaps with some regard to an actual overflow of population in contemporary Rome, calls it nevertheless 'a colonia of Roman citizens, a watch-tower of the Roman people, a bulwark against the wild tribes of Gaul'. Those words state very clearly the main object of many such foundations under Republic and Empire alike.

Another reason for the establishment of 'coloniae' may be found in the history of the dying Republic and nascent Empire. During the civil wars of Sulla, of Caesar and of Octavian, huge armies were brought into the field by the rival military chiefs. As each conflict ended, huge masses of soldiery had to be discharged almost at once. For the sake of future peace it was imperative that these men should be quickly settled in some form of civic life in which they would abide. The form chosen was the familiar form of the 'colonia'. The time-expired soldiers were treated—not altogether unreasonably—as surplus population, and they were planted out in large bodies, sometimes in existing towns which needed population or at least a loyal population, sometimes in new towns established full-grown for the purpose. This method of dealing with discharged soldiers was continued during the early Empire, though it was then employed somewhat intermittently and the 'coloniae' were oftener planted in the provinces than in Italy itself; indeed the establishment of Italian 'coloniae', as distinct from grants of colonial rank by way of honour, almost ceased after A.D. 68.

It is not easy to determine the number of such new foundations of towns in Italy. Some seventy or eighty are recorded from the early and middle periods of the Republic—previous to about 120 B.C.; Sulla added a dozen or so; Octavian (Augustus) in his earlier years established or helped to establish about thirty.[1] But these figures can hardly represent the whole facts. The one certainty is that, through the causes just

[1] See Mommsen, *Gesamm. Schriften* v. 203; Nissen, *Ital. Landeskunde* ii. 27; Kornemann in Pauly-Wissowa, *Encycl.* iv. 520 foll.

detailed, a very large number of the Italian towns were either founded full-grown or re-founded under new conditions during the later Roman Republic and the earlier Empire. Few towns in Italy developed as Rome herself developed, expanding from small beginnings in a slow continuous growth which was governed by convenience and opportunism and untouched by any new birth or systematic reconstruction.

Coincident with these processes of urban expansion, we find, in many towns which can be connected with the later Republic or the Empire, examples of a definite type of town-planning. This type has obvious analogies with earlier Italy and with the town-planning of the Greek world, but is also in certain respects distinct from either. The town areas with which we have now to deal are small squares or oblongs; they are divided by two main streets into four parts and by other and parallel streets into square or oblong house-blocks ('insulae'), and the rectangular scheme is carried through with some geometrical precision. The 'insulae', whatever their shape—square or oblong—are fairly uniform throughout. Only, those which line the north side of the E. and W. street are often larger than the rest (pp. 88, 125).[1] The two main streets appear to follow some method of orientation connected with augural science. As a rule, one of them runs north and south, the other east and west, and now and again the latter street seems to point to the spot where the sun rises

[1] Modern plans seem sometimes to imply that the 'insulae' which abutted on the walls were also abnormally large. That is because the corresponding modern blocks often include, with the original 'insula', the space between it and the wall, and also the wall itself which has been disused and built over.

above the horizon on the dawn of some day important in the history of the town.[1]

The public buildings of these towns are in general somewhat small and arranged with little attempt at processional or architectural splendour; they seldom dominate or even cross the scheme of streets. Open spaces are rare; the Forum, which corresponds to the Greek Agora, contains, like that, a paved open court, but this court is almost as much enclosed as the cloister of a mediaeval church or the quadrangle of a mediaeval college. Theatre and amphitheatre[2] might, no doubt, reach huge dimensions, but externally they were more often massive than ornamental and the amphitheatre often stood outside the city walls. Here and there a triumphal arch spanned a road where it approached a town, and provided the only architectural vista to be seen in most of these Roman towns.

Dimensions, of course, varied. There was no normal size for an infant town. Some, when first established, covered little more than 30 acres, the area of mediaeval Warwick. Others were four or five times as spacious; they were twice or nearly twice as large as mediaeval Oxford, no mean city in thirteenth-century England. Most of them, doubtless, grew beyond their first limits; a few spread as far as a square mile, twice the extent of mediaeval London. Similarly the 'insulae' varied from town to town. In one, Timgad, they were only 70 to 80 ft. square. Often they measured 75 to 80 yds. square, rather

[1] See on this point some remarks by W. Barthel, *Bonner Jahrbücher*, cxx. 101–108.

[2] In western Europe the provincial Roman amphitheatre averaged 45 × 70 yds. for its arena.

more than an acre, as at Florence, Turin, Pavia, Piacenza.[1] Occasionally they were larger, but they seldom exceeded three acres, and their average fell below the prevalent practice of modern chess-board planning.

In most towns, though not in all, the dimensions of the 'insulae' show a common element. In length or in breadth or in both, they usually approximate to 120 ft. or some multiple of that. The figure is significant. The unit of Roman land-surveying, the 'iugerum', was a rectangular space of 120 by 240 Roman feet—in English feet a tiny trifle less—and it seems to follow that 'insulae' were often laid out with definite reference to the 'iugerum'. The divisions may not have always been mathematically correct; our available plans are seldom good enough to let us judge of that,[2] and we do not know whether we ought to count the surface of the streets with the measurement of the 'insulae'. But the general practice seems clear, and it extended even to Britain (p. 129), and though blocks forming exactly a 'iugerum' or a half 'iugerum' are rare, the Italian land-measure certainly affected the civilization of the provincial towns.

In this system perhaps the most peculiar feature is the intermixture of square and oblong 'insulae'. It is not merely the variation which can be traced in Priene (fig. 5), where some blocks are rather more square or

[1] For Florence and Turin see below; for Piacenza, the plans on the scale of 1 : 1000 and 1 : 5000 in L. Buroni's *Acque potabili di Piacenza* (1895).

[2] Silchester and Timgad are the only two sites which have been planned well enough to provide accurate measurements. The large modern town-plans (e.g. of Turin, p. 86) are useful, but inadequate to our purpose; for one thing, they often exaggerate the width of the streets. One really needs actual measurements made on the spot.

oblong than others, but where all approach the same norm. The Roman towns which we are now considering show two varieties of house-blocks. Sometimes the blocks are square; sometimes, perhaps more often, they are oblong approximating to a square, like the blocks of Priene. But in a few cases, as at Naples among the more ancient, and at Carthage among the later foundations, they are oblong and the oblongs are very long and narrow.

It is hard to detect any principle underlying the use of these various forms. No doubt differences of historical origin are ultimately the causes of the mixture. But our present knowledge does not reveal these origins. The evidence is, indeed, contradictory at every point. If the Graeco-Macedonian fashion be quoted as precedent for square or squarish 'insulae', the Terremare show the same. If the theoretical scheme of the earlier Roman camp seemed based on the long narrow oblong, the actual remains of legionary encampments of the second century B.C. at Numantia include many squares. If one part of Pompeii exhibits oblongs, another part is made up of squares. If Piacenza, first founded in north Italy about 183 B.C., and founded again a hundred and fifty years later, is laid out in squares, its coeval neighbour Modena prefers the oblong. If the old Greek city of Naples embodies an extreme type of oblong, so does the later Augustan Carthage (pp. 100, 113). In the historic period, it would seem, no sharp line was drawn, or felt to exist, between the various types of 'insulae'. In the main, the square or squarish-oblong was preferred. Local accidents, such as the convenience of the site at Carthage, led to occasional adoption of the narrower oblong.

The Roman land-surveyors, it is true, distinguished the square and the oblong in a very definite way. The square, they alleged, was proper to the Italian land or to such provincial soil as enjoyed the privilege of being taxed—or freed from taxation—on the Italian scale. The oblong they connected with the ordinary tax-paying soil of the provinces. This distinction, however, was not carried out even in the agrarian surveys with which these writers were especially concerned,[1] and it applies still less to the towns. No doubt it is a fiction of the office. It would be only human nature if the surveyors, finding both forms in use, should invent a theory to account for them.

The system sketched in the preceding paragraphs seems, as has been said (p. 73), to have sprung from a fusion of Greek or Graeco-Macedonian with Italian customs. Roman town-planning, like Roman art, was recast under Hellenistic influence and thus gained mathematical precision and symmetry. When this happened is doubtful. Foreign scholars often ascribe it to Augustus and find a special connexion between the first emperor and the chess-board town-plan. But the architect Vitruvius, who dedicated his book to Augustus and who gives some brief notice to town-planning, urges strongly that towns should not be laid out on the chess-board pattern, but rather on an eight-sided or (as we might call it) star-shaped plan.[2] He would hardly have denounced a scheme which had been specially taken up by his patron, nor indeed does his criticism of the

[1] Schulten, *Bonner Jahrbücher*, ciii. 23, and references given there.

[2] i. 5 (21), 6 (28, 29).

chess-board system sound as if he were denouncing a novelty in Italian building.

On the other hand there seems no great difficulty in the idea that the regularization of the old Italian town-plan by Greek influence took place spontaneously in the late Republic. We cannot, indeed, date the change. It must remain doubtful whether it came by degrees or all at once,[1] and whether the right-angled plans of towns like Aquileia [2] or Piacenza belonged to their first foundation, i.e. to about 180 B.C., or to later rearrangements. But it seems reasonable to believe that a Graeco-Italian rectangular fashion of town-planning did supersede an earlier, irregular, Italian style, and had become supreme before the end of the Republic.

[1] Perhaps about 180 B.C., Mommsen, *Roman Hist.* iii. 206.

[2] Aquileia was set up in 181 B.C. to guard the north-east gate of Italy, and was reinforced in 169. Its remains, so far as excavated, show a rectangular plan of oblong 'insulae'—some of $1\frac{1}{2}$ acres (74 by 94 yards), some larger—while, till its downfall, about A.D. 450, we hear no word of refoundation or wholesale rebuilding. But if its original area be the space of 70 acres which is usually assigned, that is not rectangular but a square somewhat askew, which fits very badly with the rectangular street-plan, and one would incline to ascribe the latter to a later date. See Maionica, *Fundkarte von Aquileia.*

## CHAPTER VII

### INSTANCES OF ITALIAN TOWN-PLANS

THE preceding chapters have dealt with the origins and general character of the Italian town-plan. We pass now to the remains which it has left in its own home, in Italy. These are many. In one city indeed, the greatest of all, no town-planning can be detected. Like Athens and Sparta, Rome shows that conservatism which marks so many capital cities. No part of it, so far as we know, was laid out on a rectangular or indeed on any plan.[1] It grew as it could. Its builders, above all its imperial builders, cared much for spectacular effects and architectural pomp. Even in late Republican times the gloomy mass of the Tabularium and the temples of the Capitol must have towered above the Forum in no mere accidental stateliness, and imperial Rome contained many buildings in many quarters to show that it was the capital of an Empire. But for town-planning we must go elsewhere.

The sources of our knowledge are twofold. In a few cases archaeological excavation has laid bare the paving of Roman streets or the foundation of Roman house-blocks. More often mediaeval and modern streets seem to follow ancient lines and the ancient town-plan, or a part of it, survives in use to-day. Such survivals are especially common in the north of Italy. It is not,

[1] The traces of prehistoric planning detected by some writers in Rome are very dubious.

indeed, possible to gather a full list of them. He who would do that needs a longer series of good town-maps and good local histories than exist at present; he needs, too, a wider knowledge of mediaeval Italian history and a closer personal acquaintance with modern Italian towns, than a classical scholar can attempt. But much can be learnt even from our limited material.[1]

The evidence of the streets needs, however, to be checked in every case. It would be rash to assume a Roman origin for an Italian town simply because its streets are old and their plan rectangular. There are many rectangular towns of mediaeval or modern origin. Such is Terra Nova, near the ancient Gela in Sicily, built by Frederick Stupor Mundi early in the thirteenth century. Such, too, Livorno, built by the Medici in the sixteenth century. Such, too, the many little military colonies of the Italian Republics, dotted over parts of northern and middle Italy. Often it is easy to prove that, despite their chess-board plans, these towns do not stand on Roman sites. Often the inquiry leads into regions remote from the study of ancient history.

Fortunately, enough examples can be identified as Roman to serve our purpose. Some of these occur in the Lombardy plain where, both under the Republic and at the outset of the Empire, many 'coloniae' were

[1] See the seventeenth century Atlases of Blaeu, Janssons, and others, the modern maps prepared by Grassellini and others about 1840–50 (some on the scale 1 : 4,000), and in particular the *Atlante geografico* of Attilio Zuccagni-Orlandini (Firenze, 1844), and the recent town-maps of various Italian cities (mostly about 1 : 10,500). Different maps of the same town sometimes differ much in their detail. The Italian Government maps of the largest scale (1 : 25,000) are small for our present purpose and have been issued mainly for northern Italy.

planted full-grown and where town-life on the Roman model was otherwise developed. Not all these towns survive to-day; not all of the survivors retain clear traces of their Roman town-plan; in nine cases, at least, the streets seem unmistakably to follow Roman lines. Four of the nine date from early days; in the late third and the early second centuries (218–183 B.C.), Piacenza, Bologna, Parma, and Modena, were built as new towns with the rank of 'colonia'. The first three of these were later refounded, about 40–20 B.C.—whether their streets were then laid out afresh is an open question—and Turin and Brescia were added. In addition, Verona, Pavia, and Como won municipal status in or before this later date, though when or how they came to be laid out symmetrically is not certain.[1] And there are other less certain examples.

Other instances, but not so many, may be quoted from south of the Apennines. At Florence, for example, and at Lucca 'coloniae' were planted full-grown and the street-plans still record the fact. At Naples, at Herculaneum, perhaps at Sorrento,[2] proofs survive of similar planning. But the towns of central Italy were in great part more ancient than the era of precise town-planning, and many of them were perched in true Italian fashion on lofty crags—*praeruptis oppida saxis*—which gave no

[1] Milan (Mediolanium), once the chief Roman town of north Italy, is usually stated to preserve to-day no trace of Roman street-planning. But the line of the Via Manzoni, Via Margherita, and Via Nerino (cutting the Ambrosian Library) seems really to represent one of its main streets, and the line of the Fulcorino and Corso di Porta Romana the other, while one or two traces of 'insulae' can be detected near the Ambrosian Library. The town was destroyed in A.D. 539 and again in 1162, and more survivals cannot be expected.

[2] Beloch, *Campanien*, p. 252.

room for square or oblong house-blocks. In the period of the dying Republic and nascent Empire fewer 'coloniae' were planted here than in the north, while in much of southern Italy towns have in all ages been comparatively rare.

In the towns just noted we can trace many, though not all, of the original house-blocks. Usually the blocks are square or nearly so, as at Turin, Verona, Pavia, Piacenza, Florence, Lucca. Less often they are long and even narrow rectangles, as at Modena, and Sorrento, and above all Naples, and as usual it is not easy to understand the reason for the difference (p. 80).

### *Turin* (fig. 15).

Of all the examples of Roman town-planning known to us in Italy, Turin is by far the most famous.[1] Here the streets have survived almost intact, and excavations have confirmed the truth of the survival by revealing both the ancient road-metalling and the ancient town-walls and gates. Turin, Augusta Taurinorum, began about 28 B.C. as a 'colonia' planted by Augustus. Its walls enclosed an oblong of about 745 × 695 metres (127 acres).[2] The sides are represented (1) on the

[1] Carlo Promis, *Storia dell' antico Torino* (Torino, 1869); Alfredo d'Andrade, *Relazione dell' ufficio regionale per la conservazione dei monumenti del Piemonte*, 1883–91 (Torino, 1899); Schultze, *Bonner Jahrbücher*, cxviii. 339; Barthel, *ibid.* cxx. 105; Pianta di Torino (1–10,000), by G. B. Paravia.

[2] I take these figures from the plan of Paravia, which is said to be the most correct plan of Turin at present available. Promis gives smaller dimensions, 720 × 670 m., and he measured from what is now known to be a point too far to the east (the Via Accademia delle Scienze) instead of from the west front of the Palazzo Madama; he has, however, been usually followed. Other maps give other dimensions, Orlandini (1844), 758 × 780 m.; Vallardi (1869), 680 × 740 m.;

north by the Via Giulio, in the western part of which the southern edge of the street actually coincides with the line of the Roman town-wall, while further east the Porta Palatina enshrines an ancient gate; (2) on the west by the Via della Consolata, and the Via Siccardi, the east side of which latter street seems to stand upon the Roman town-wall; and (3) on the south by the Via della Cernaia and Via Teresa, the north side of which stands over the Roman southern town-wall. (4) The east wall agrees with no existing street but may be represented by a line drawn through the Carignano Theatre and the western front of the Palazzo Madama, which contains the actual towers of the Roman east gate.[1] The north-west corner, uncovered in 1884, is a sharp right angle. This feature recurs at Aosta and at Laibach (pp. 90, 116), both founded, like Turin, in the Augustan age, and seems to belong to that period: later, it gave place to the rounded angle visible at Timgad (p. 109) and in many Roman forts of the middle Empire.

Of the interior buildings of the town little is known. The Forum perhaps stood near the present Palazzo di Città, and the Theatre was traced in 1899 in the north-east corner of the town, occupying apparently, a complete insula;[2] of the private houses nothing definite seems to be recorded.

Maggi (1876), 730 × 800 m.; Ashby (Art. 'Turin' in *Encycl. Britannica*) gives 2,526 × 2,330 ft. which must be too large. I reproduce here (fig. 15) the plan of Orlandini, since it shows well the extent of street-survivals in Turin before the great modern rebuildings or expansions.

[1] d'Andrade, *Relazione*, pp. 8–20; *Notizie degli Scavi*, 1885, pp. 173, 271, and 1902, p. 277.

[2] *Notizie*, 1903, p. 3.

But the street-plan has survived intact, except in two outlying corners. The town was divided up into square or nearly square blocks, of which there were nine counting from east to west and eight from north to south. Most of these 'insulae' measured about 80 yds. square.[1] A few were larger, 80 × 120 yds. ; these were ranged along the north side of the street now called Via Garibaldi (formerly Dora Grossa), which represents the Roman main street between the east and west gates—in the language of the Roman land-surveyors, the *decumanus maximus*. This street cut the town into two equal halves. The other divisions of the town were no less symmetrical. But, as there were nine 'insulae' from east to west, the main north and south street could not bisect the town. Indeed, the south gate seems to have had five house-blocks west of it and four east of it, while the Porta Palatina stands further west, with six blocks on the west side of it. The north and south gates, therefore, are not opposite.[2] Whether this was the original plan is not clear, nor is the age of the surviving walls and gates quite certain ; the bonding

[1] An insula is mentioned in *Notizie*, 1901, p. 391, which measured 74 × 80 metres. It is likely that there were small unevennesses in the ancient as there are in the modern house-blocks. The 'insulae' which abutted on the town-walls are represented to-day by unduly large blocks, oblong rather than square, but these latter contain not only the areas of the Roman 'insulae' in question, but also the space between them and the town-walls and the lines of the wall themselves (p. 77).

[2] This failure in symmetry recurs in one or two other Roman towns as probably at Timgad (p. 109) and at Cologne (E. and W. gates), at Silchester and Caerwent, but it may sometimes be the result of alteration. Occasionally it appears in military sites (Ritterling, *Lager bei Hofheim*, p. 29 *note*). It is presumably a mere matter of convenience ; no superstition attaches to it such as that which led the Chinese not to put their gates opposite each other (p. 148).

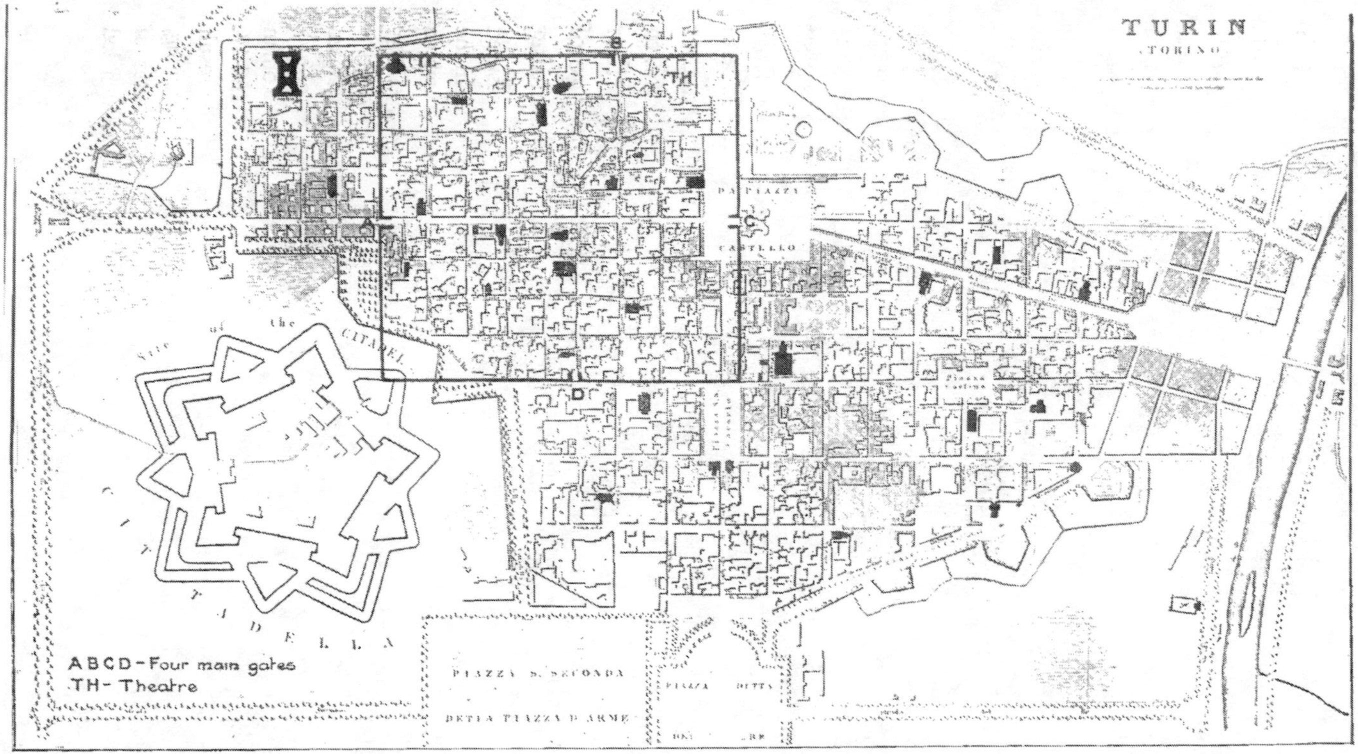


FIG. 15. FROM A PLAN OF 1844.

courses in some of the masonry of the walls does not seem Augustan. But the street plan may unhesitatingly be assigned to the first establishment of the town, about 28 B.C. Since, it has been extended far beyond the Roman walls. Nearly all modern Turin has been laid out, bit by bit, in imitation and continuation of the original Roman lines.

*Aosta* (fig. 16).

Another example of an Italian town-plan, from the same date and district as Turin, is supplied by Augusta Praetoria, now Aosta, some fifty miles north of Turin in the Dora Baltea Valley, not far from the foot of Mont Blanc.[1] Aosta was founded by Augustus in 25 B.C. on a hitherto empty spot, to provide homes for time-expired soldiers and to serve as a quasi-fortress in an important Alpine valley. Its first inhabitants were 3,000 men discharged from the Praetorian Guard, with their wives and children; its population may have numbered at the outset some 15,000 free persons, besides slaves. The town, as it is known to us from excavation and observation, formed a rectangle 620 yds. long and 780 yds. wide, and covered an area of about 100 acres (fig. 16). The walls formed sharp right angles at the corners, as at Turin. Within the walls were an amphitheatre, a theatre, public baths, a structure covering nearly 2 acres and interpreted as a granary or (perhaps more correctly) as a cistern,[2] and private houses as yet unexplored. Beneath the chief streets were sewers, by which indeed these streets were mainly traced.

[1] C. Promis, *Antichità di Aosta* (Torino, 1862), with plan, plate 3, dating from 1838; *Notizie degli Scavi*, 1899, p. 108, with a later plan, but lacking a scale; Nissen, *Ital. Landeskunde*, ii. 171.

[2] Durm *Baukunst der Römer*, p. 458.

The whole was divided by a regular network of streets into rectangular blocks. According to the latest plan of the site, there were sixteen blocks, nearly identical in shape and averaging 145 × 180 yds. ($5\frac{1}{2}$ acres). That, however, is an incredible area for

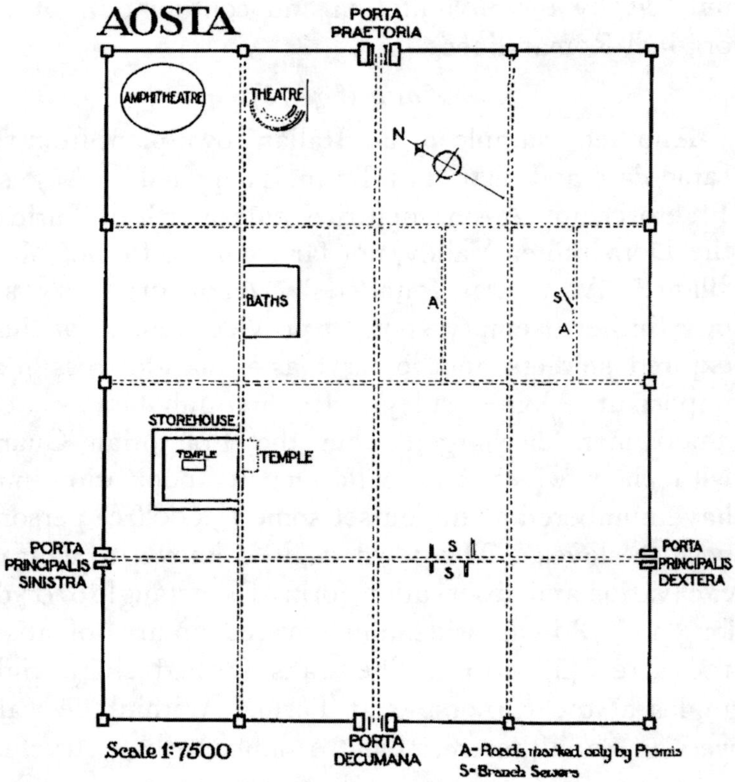


FIG. 16. AOSTA.

single house-blocks, and it is to be noted that Promis shows two further roads (A, A in fig. 16). If these are survivals of other such roads, Aosta may have contained thirty-two oblong 'insulae', each nearly 220 × 540 ft., or even sixty-four smaller and squarer 'insulae', measuring half that size.[1] Four gates gave entrance; those in the two longer sides which face north-west and south-east, are curiously far from the centre and indeed close to the south-western end of the town. It is, of course, impossible to determine, without spade-work, which of the recognizable buildings of Aosta date from the foundation of the place in 25 B.C. But the general internal scheme and the symmetrical and practically 'chess-board' pattern of streets must date from the first foundation.[2]

### *Florence* (fig. 17).

A yet more interesting instance of a Roman town-plan preserved in many streets may be found in Florence.[3] In Roman times Florence was a 'colonia'. When this 'colonia' was planted is very doubtful. Perhaps the age of Sulla (90–80 B.C.) is the likeliest date; all that is actually certain is that the founda-

[1] Promis, p. 140; his plan has no proper scale. There seems no decisive evidence and the modern streets of Aosta do not help us.

[2] The town of Concordia in north-east Italy, where Augustus planted a 'colonia', doubtless of discharged soldiers, is said to have possessed a ground-plan of oblong blocks very like that of Augusta Praetoria. But this plan rests mainly on the authority of a workman who apparently did not know how to read or write (he is described as 'analfabeta') and I therefore omit it here. See *Notizie degli Scavi*, 1880, p. 412, and Plate XII (the text gives no dimensions and the plan lacks a scale), and compare 1882, p. 426, and 1894, p. 399.

[3] On Roman and early mediaeval Florence see Villani, *Cronica* (written about 1345, published 1845), i. 61, 89, 120; R. Davidsohn, *Geschichte von Florenz* and *Forschungen* (Berlin, 1886); L. A. Milani, *Notizie degli Scavi*, 1887, p. 129; plan of the Centro in 1427 by Comm. Guido Carocci, *Studi storici sul Centro di Firenze* (Florence, 1889); *Monumenti antichi*, vi. 15. Nissen (*Ital. Landeskunde*, ii. 296) fixes its area at 400 × 600 m., about 58 acres.

tion was made before the end of the first century A.D. This 'colonia', like others, was laid out in chess-board fashion, and vestiges of its streets survive in the Centro which forms the heart of the present town. The Centro of Florence, as we see it to-day, is very

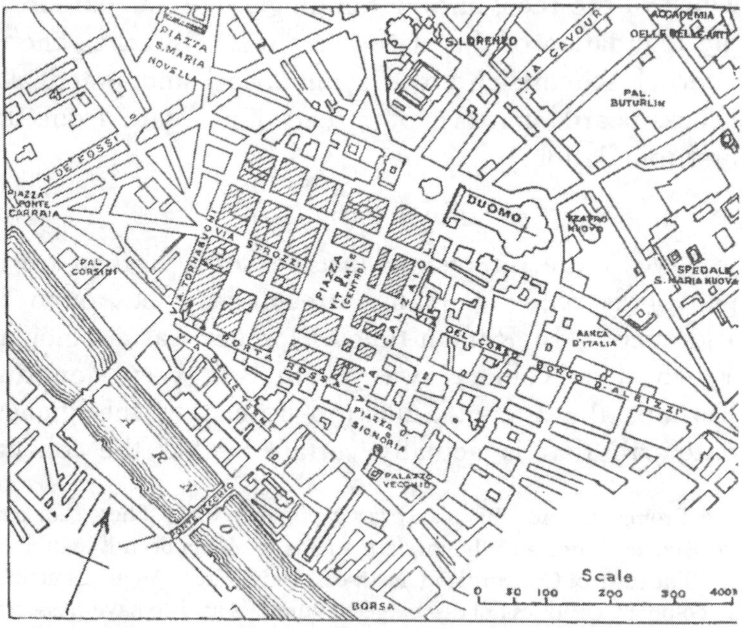


FIG. 17 A. FLORENCE, SINCE THE REBUILDING OF THE CENTRAL PORTION (Centro shaded).

modern. It was, indeed, laid out a generation ago by Italian architects who designed the broad streets crossing at right angles which form its characteristic. But this 'Haussmannization' revived, consciously or unconsciously, an old arrangement. The plan of Florence in 1427 shows a group of twenty unmistakable 'insulae', each of them about $1\frac{1}{8}$ acre in area, that is, very similar in size to the 'insulae' of Turin. This group is bounded by the modern streets Tornabuoni on the west, Porta

Rossa on the south, Calzaioli on the east, Teatina on the north; it covers a rectangle of some 305 × 327 yds., not quite 21 acres.

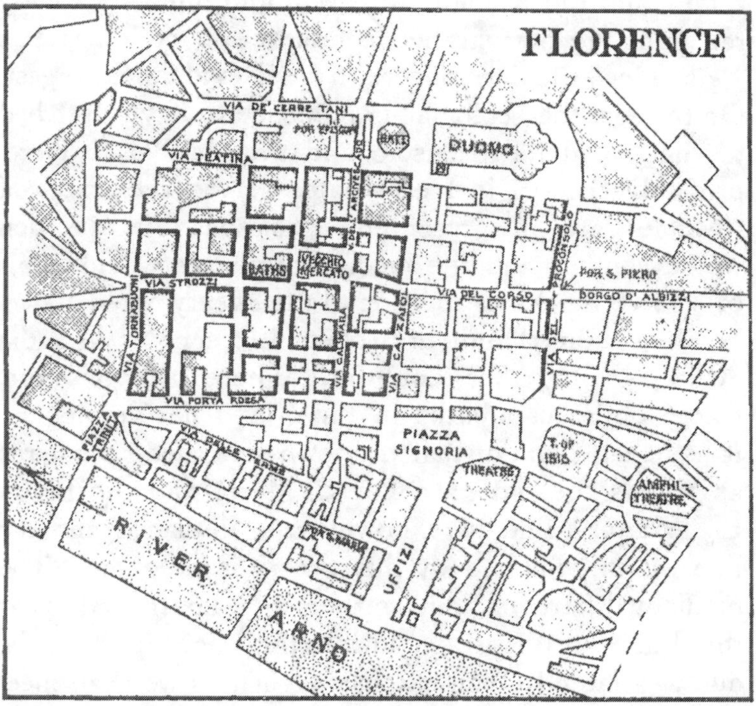


FIG. 17 B. FLORENCE ABOUT 1795, FROM L. BARDI.
The chief streets which seem to have preserved Roman lines are marked in black.

The original Roman town presumably extended beyond these narrow limits. But it is not easy to fix its area, nor are unmistakable 'insulae' to be detected outside them. On the west the Via Tornabuoni seems to have marked the Roman limit, as it does to-day. On the north, a probable line is given by the gateway, Por

Episcopi, which once spanned the passage—now an open space—on the east side of the Archbishop's Palace (plan 17 B). That gateway stood between the Via Teatina and the next street to the north, the Via dei Cerretani, and the Roman north wall and ditch apparently ran along the intervals between these two modern streets—as indeed the lines of certain mediaeval lanes suggest. On the east the 'colonia' is supposed to have stretched to the Via del Proconsolo and the old Por S. Piero, probably the original east gate. Here the traces of 'insulae' are ill preserved; the space in question would contain, and the mediaeval streets would admit of, twelve blocks in addition to the twenty noted above.

The southern limit of Roman Florence towards the Arno is altogether doubtful. There are, or were, traces of Roman baths in the Via delle Terme, and it has been thought that the town stretched riverwards as far as the old gate Por S. Maria and the Piazza S. Trinità. The gate, however, is ill-placed and the line of wall implied by this theory is irregular. The mediaeval streets point rather to a south wall near the Via Porta Rossa. The baths might perhaps be due to a later Roman extension, such as we shall meet at Timgad (p. 113). The Por S. Maria may even be due to one of the reconstructions of Florence in the Middle Ages. At the end we must admit that without further evidence the limits of Roman Florence cannot be fixed for certain. But the limits indicated above give the not unsuitable dimensions of 46 acres (380 × 590 yds.), while the history of the twenty indubitable insulae of the Centro remains full of interest. We see here, as clearly as anywhere in the Roman world, how the regular Roman plan has gradually been distorted by encroachments and how, even in its irregularity, it has had power to drive modern builders towards its ancient fashion.

Of the interior of the Roman town little is known. The streets now called Strozzi and Speziali plainly preserve the Roman main street from east to west, while the Via Calimara overlies that which ran from north to south. Where these crossed was the mediaeval Mercato Vecchio, now enlarged into a patriotic Piazza Vittorio Emmanuele; here we may put the Roman forum, and here too, by the former church of S. Maria in Campidoglio, was the temple of Capitoline Juppiter. There were also theatres, a shrine of Isis, and, outside the Roman limit, an amphitheatre still discernible in the curves of certain streets (plan 17 B). However small Florentia was, it possessed the true elements of the Roman town.

### *Lucca* (fig. 18).

A good parallel to Florence may be found at Lucca, the ancient Luca, where again the streets preserve a rectangular pattern without showing clearly what was its full extent. Luca is said to have been founded as a 'colonia' in 177 B.C., but the statement is of doubtful truth. Certainly it was a 'municipium' in Cicero's days, and a little later, in the period 40–20 B.C., it received the rank of 'colonia' and many colonists, taken (as an inscription says) from discharged soldiers of Legions VII and XXVI. Whether the surviving traces of town-planning date from this latter event or from some earlier age is not easy to say. But of the street-plan there can be no doubt, though its original size is uncertain. A rectangular area about 700 yds from east to west and 360 yds. from north to south is divided into fifteen square or squarish 'insulae' arranged in three rows. Each insula is about 3 acres, but those of the middle row are larger than the rest (150 × 150 yds.). The Via S. Croce which runs along the

**LUCCA**

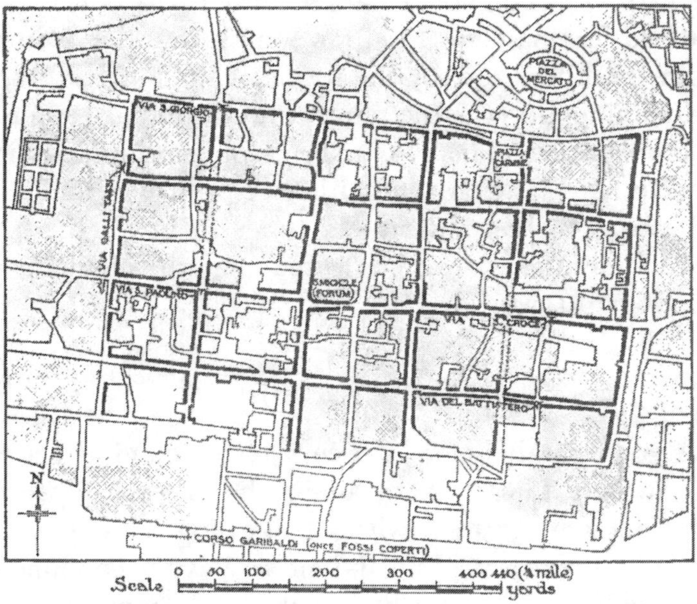


FIG. 18. The streets which preserve Roman lines are marked in black.

south side of this row was perhaps the main east and west thoroughfare of the town, the 'decumanus maximus', so that the larger 'insulae' correspond to those which appear in the same position at Turin and elsewhere (p. 88).

Whether there were other 'insulae' besides the fifteen is doubtful. On the east there were certainly none : the two narrow parallel streets at the east end of the area just described are obviously due to a growth of houses along the line of the original east wall. The other limits are more obscure. Probably the north and west walls stood a little outside of the Via Galli Tassi (once S. Pellegrino) and the Via S. Giorgio, but there may well have been a row of insulae, now obliterated, south of the Via del Battistero. One or two interior buildings are known. The Forum appears to have stood where is now the Piazza S. Michele in Foro; close by was a temple; in the north-eastern quarter, at the Piazza del Carmine, was probably the theatre; near it but outside the walls was the amphitheatre, its outlines still visible in the Piazza del Mercato (110 × 80 yds. in greatest dimensions).[1]

### *Herculaneum* (fig. 19).

To these examples from north Italy may be added two from the south, Herculaneum and Naples. Herculaneum had much the same early history as its more important neighbour Pompeii. First an Oscan settlement, then Etruscan, then Samnite, it passed later under Roman rule. After the Social Wars (89 B.C.) it appears as a 'municipium'; of its history from that date till its destruction (A.D. 79) we know next to nothing. But excavations, commenced in the eighteenth century and now long suspended, have thrown light on its ground-plan.[2] This was a

[1] Plan by P. Sinibaldi, 1843, 1 : 4,000. *Notizie degli Scavi*, 1906, p. 117, &c. Nissen (*Ital. Landeskunde*, ii. 288) gives the area as 800 × 1,200 metres, which seems much too large.

[2] M. Ruggiero, *Scavi di Ercolano* (Naples, 1885), plates ii and xii; Beloch, *Campanien*, pp. 215 foll.; Nissen, *Ital. Landeskunde*, ii. 759;

rectangular pattern of oblong house-blocks, measuring 54 × 89 yds., or in some cases a little more, and divided by streets varying from 15 to 30 ft. in width which ran at right angles or parallel to one another. Only a part of the town has been as yet unearthed. In that a broad colonnaded main street ran from north-west to south-east; on the north-east side of this street stood a row of house-blocks with a structure taken to be a Basilica, and on the south-west of it were ten

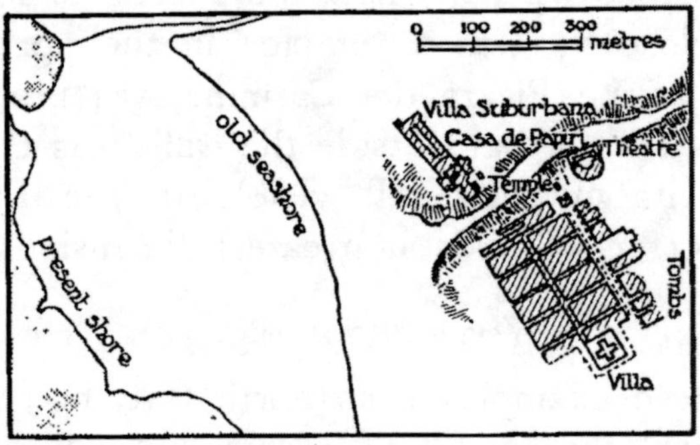


FIG. 19. HERCULANEUM.

house-blocks, one of which includes some public baths. At the north end of this area are a theatre and temple, at the south end two large structures which have been called temples but are more like large private houses; on the east (according to the eighteenth-century searchers) are graves.

How much of the town has been uncovered, how much still lies hidden beneath the lava which overflowed it in A.D. 79, is disputed. Of its town walls and gates no trace has yet been found. But nearly

Waldstein and Shoobridge, *Herculaneum* (London, 1908), pp. 60 foll.; E. R. Barker, *Buried Herculaneum* (1908); Gall in Pauly-Wissowa, viii. (1912) 532–48.

all its public buildings seem to be known; the graves on the east side, if correctly mapped by their discoverers and if coeval with the streets and houses, leave no room for further 'insulae' in that direction, while the great country-house called the 'Casa dei Papiri' plainly stood outside the town on the north-west. From these facts one modern writer has calculated that Herculaneum was less than a quarter of a mile long, less than 350 yds. broad, and less than 26 acres in extent—in short, not a sixth part of Pompeii. These measures are probably too small. The 'Basilica' on the north side of the main street cannot have stood on the extreme edge of the town. There must have been not three but four rows of house-blocks from south-west to north-east; the graves once noted in this quarter must be older than our Herculaneum or otherwise unconnected with it. The whole town must have been 40 or 45 rather than 25 acres in area. Even so it is a little town. The unenthusiastic references to it in ancient literature are, after all, truthful. Apart from the great villa outside it—possibly an imperial residence—it hardly deserved, or to-day deserves, to be excavated at the extraordinary cost which its excavation would involve.

The date of its planning is as doubtful as the extent of its area. One recent writer, Nissen, has suggested that it was reconstructed after an earthquake in A.D. 63 and was hardly completed before the eruption of 79. The earthquake is well attested. But it cannot possibly have wrecked the town so utterly as to cause wholesale rebuilding on new lines, and an inscription points rather to the time of Augustus. One Marcus Nonius Balbus (the text runs) built 'a basilica, gates and a

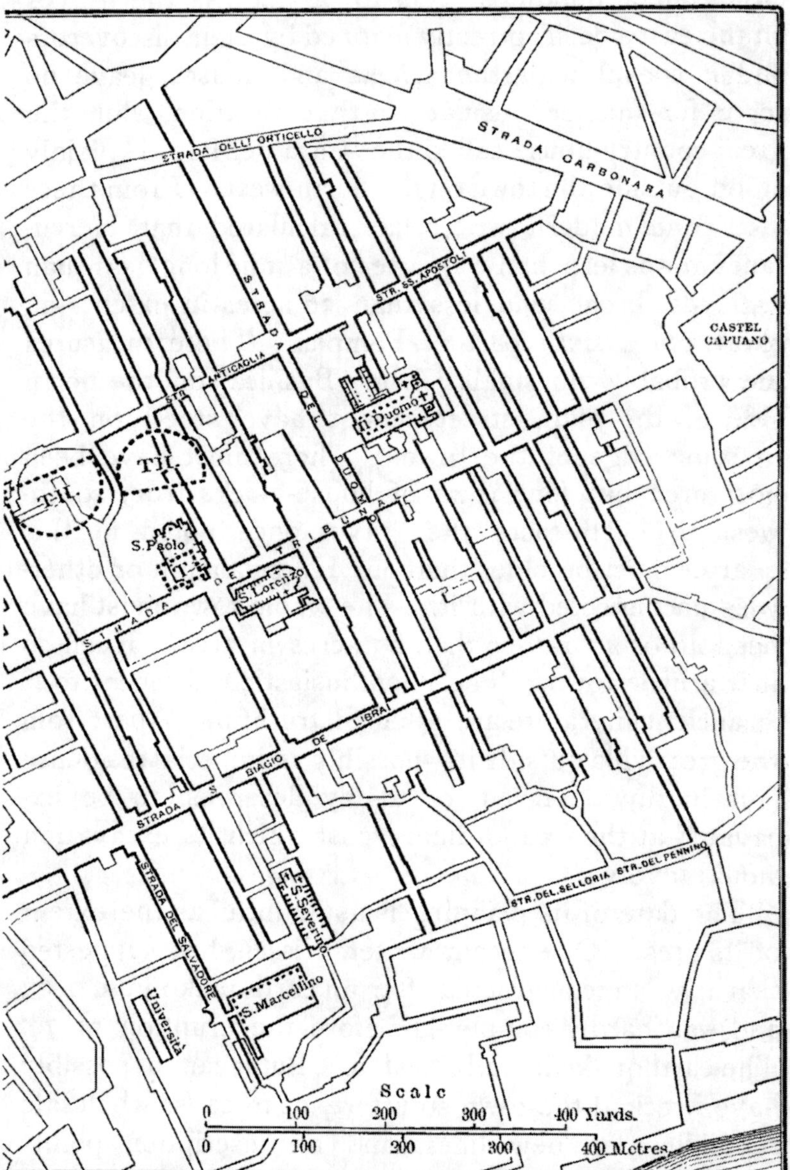


APTED FROM A PLAN OF 1865. (TH = Theatre, T = Temple.)

Greek civilization. A writer of the early first century after Christ, Strabo, states that abundant traces of Greek life survived there, 'gymnasia, and athletic schools, and tribal divisions, and Greek names even for Roman things.' Even later Tacitus calls it a 'Greek city', and Greek was still used for official inscriptions there in the third century.

This Neapolis town had, as certain existing streets declare, a peculiar form of town-planning. The area covered by these streets is an irregular space of 250 acres in the heart of the modern city, about 850 yds. from north to south and 1,000 yds. from east to west.[1] In Roman days three straight streets ran parallel from east to west and a large number of smaller streets, twenty or so, ran at right angles to them from north to south. The house-blocks enclosed by these streets were all of similar size and shape, a thin oblong of 35 × 180 metres (39 × 198 yds.). Some of the public buildings naturally trespassed on to more than one 'insula'; a theatre appears indeed to have stretched over parts of three. In general, the oblongs seem to have been laid out with great regularity and the angles are right angles, though the 'insulae' in the northern and southern rows of house-blocks cannot have been fully rectangular and symmetrical.

This town-plan of Naples differs from any of those noted above. Its blocks are narrower than those in any Italian town, unless in Modena, and while they resemble the 'insulae' of the sixth region of Pompeii (fig. 13), are far more regular than those. Almost

[1] The limits are the Castel Capuano on the east, the Strada dell' Orticello on the north, the church of S. Pietro a Majella on the west, and on the south the churches of S. Marcellino and S. Severino.

the only close parallel is that of Roman Carthage (fig. 24). As Naples was by origin and character a Greek city, these narrow oblongs have been supposed to represent a Greek arrangement. They do not, however, correspond to anything that is known in the Greek lands, either of the Macedonian or of any earlier period. The conclusion is difficult to avoid that this Greek city of Naples adopted an Italian street-scheme, but laid it out with more scientific regularity than the early Italians themselves. When this occurred and why, is wholly unknown. That the result is not an unpractical form of building is shown by the fact that similar long and narrow house-blocks are a characteristic feature of modern Liverpool, though they seldom occur in other English towns, unless intermixed with square and other blocks.

# CHAPTER VIII

## Roman Provincial Town-plans. I

The provinces, and above all the western provinces of the Roman Empire, tell us even more than Italy about Roman town-planning. But they tell it in another way. They contain many towns which were founded full-grown, or re-founded and at the same time rebuilt, and which were in either case laid out on the Roman plan. But the modern successors of these towns have rarely kept the network of their ancient streets in recognizable detail. Though walls, gates, temples, baths, palaces, amphitheatres still stand stubbornly erect amidst a flood of modern dwellings, they are but the islands which mark a submerged area. The paths and passages by which men once moved across that area have vanished beneath the waves and cannot be recovered from any survey of these visible fragments. There is hardly one modern town in all the European and African provinces of the Roman Empire which still uses any considerable part of its ancient street-plan. In our own country there is no single case. In Gaul and Germany, two or three streets in Cologne and one or two in Trier are the sole survivals.[1] In Illyricum there is no example unless possibly at Belgrade. In the Spanish peninsula the town of Braga in northern

[1] For Orange see p. 107. Nîmes may possibly retain one or two streets of the Roman Nemausus, but it is very doubtful; see Menard's map of 1752. See further in general p. 142.

Portugal seems to stand alone. In Roman Africa—Tunis, Algiers and Morocco—no instance has survived the Arab conquest.[1]

If, however, survivals of ancient streets are as rare in the provinces as they are common in Italy, the provinces yield other evidence unknown to Italy. In these lands, and above all in Africa, the sites of many Roman towns have lain desolate and untouched since Roman days, waiting for the excavator to recover the unspoilt pattern of their streets. If the Roman Empire brought to certain provinces, as it unquestionably did to Africa, the happiest period in their history till almost the present day, that only makes their remains the more noteworthy and instructive. Here the new art of excavation has already achieved many and varied successes. In the western Empire one town, Silchester in Britain, has been wholly uncovered within the circuit of its walls. Others, like Caerwent in Britain or Timgad and Carthage in Africa, have been methodically examined, though the inquiries have not yet touched or perhaps can never touch their whole areas. In others again, some of which lie in the east, occasional search or even chance discoveries have shed welcome light. Our knowledge is more than enough already for the purposes of this chapter.

We can already see that the town-plan described in the foregoing pages was widely used in the provinces of the Empire. We find it in Africa, in Central and Western Europe, and indeed wherever Roman remains have been carefully excavated; we find it even in remote Britain amidst conditions which make its use

[1] Though, curiously enough, the chess-board pattern of field divisions has survived in the neighbourhood of Carthage.

seem premature. Where excavation has as yet yielded no proofs, other evidence fills the gap. In southern Gaul, as it happens, archaeological remains are unhelpful. But just there an inscription has come to light, the only one of its kind in the Roman world, which proves that one at least of the 'coloniae' of Gallia Narbonensis was laid out in rectangular oblong plots. It is clear enough that this town-plan was one of the forms through which the Italian civilization diffused itself over the western provinces.

The exact measure of its popularity is, however, hard to determine. In the east it found little entrance. There, the very similar Macedonian and Greek methods of town-planning were rooted firmly, long before Rome conquered Greece or Asia Minor or Syria or Egypt. The few town-plans which have been noted in these lands, and which may be assigned more or less conjecturally to the Roman era, seem to be Hellenic or Hellenistic rather than Italian. They show broad stately streets, colonnades, vistas, which belong to the east and not to Italy. Even in the west, the rule of the chess-board was sometimes broken. Aquincum, near Budapest, became a 'municipium' under Hadrian; its ruins, so far as hitherto planned, exhibit no true street-planning. But that may be due to its history, for it seems not to have been founded full-grown, but to have slowly developed as best it could, and to have won municipal status at the end.

Roman Africa is here, as so often, our best source of knowledge. At Timgad (p. 109), a town laid out in Roman fashion with a rigid 'chess-board' of streets was subsequently enlarged on irregular and almost chaotic lines. At Gigthi, in the south-east of Tunis, the streets around the Forum, itself rectangular enough, do not run parallel or at right angles to it or to one another.[1] At Thibilis, on the border of Tunis and Algeria, the streets, so far as they have yet been uncovered, diverge widely from the chess-board pattern.[2] One French archaeologist has even declared that most of the towns in Roman Africa lacked this pattern.[3] Our evidence is perhaps still too slight to prove or disprove that conclusion. Few African towns have been sufficiently uncovered to show the street-plan.[4] But town-life was well developed in Roman Africa. It is hardly credible that the Africans learnt all the rest of Roman city civilization and city government, and left out the planning. The individual cases of such planning which will be quoted in the following pages tell their own tale—that, while the strict rule was often broken, it was the rule.

[1] *Archives nouvelles des Missions scientifiques*, xv. 1907, fasc. 4.

[2] Plan by Joly, *Arch. Anzeiger*, 1911, p. 270, fig. 17. The plan has been thought to imply 'insulae' twice as large as those of Timgad. To me it suggests nothing so regular.

[3] Toutain, *Cités romaines de la Tunisie*, p. 79 note: 'Ce qui toutefois est incontestable, c'est que cette disposition d'une régularité artificielle, autour de deux grandes voies exactement orientées et se coupant à angle droit, est très rare dans l'Afrique romaine. Les villes de ce pays n'ont pas été toutes construites sur le même plan : chacune d'elles a, pour ainsi dire, épousé la forme de son emplacement.'

[4] There are many in which it could be traced with some ease, apparently. Thelepte, Cillium, Ammaedara, Sufetula, *Archives des Missions*, 1887, pp. 68, 121, 161–171, Simitthu, *Mémoires présentés par divers savants*, sér. I. x. 462, and Thuccabor, Tissot, *Géogr. d'Afrique*, ii. 292, seem to have visible streets, but no one has recorded them exactly. The plan of Utica, given by Tissot (*Atlas*, by Reinach, plate vi) on the authority of Daux, is open to doubt.

FIG. 21. INSCRIPTION OF ORANGE.

(From the *Comptes-rendus de l'Académie des Inscriptions.*)

Plot (*meris*) I (*lost*) . . .

Plot II . . . perpetual lessee (*manceps*) C. Naevius Rusticus: surety for him C. Vesidius Quadratus. Fronting the Kardo.

Plot III, frontage of $34\frac{1}{2}$ feet and Plot IV, frontage of 35 feet; ground rent (?), $69\frac{1}{2}$ denarii (*in margin*). Yearly rent II . . . (?). Lessee and surety, as above. Fronting the Kardo.

Plot V, frontage $55\frac{1}{2}$ feet, and Plot VI, next to the Ludus (gladiators' school), frontage 75 feet . . .

### *Orange* (fig. 21).

The case which deserves the first place stands by itself. It is the one piece of written evidence (as distinct from structural remains) which has survived from Roman town-planning. Curiously enough, it was found not in Italy but in a province, and a province which, for all its wealth of Roman buildings, has not yet revealed the smallest structural proof of Roman town-planning. In April 1904 a scrap of inscribed marble, little more than 18 in. broad and high, was dug up at Orange, in southern France, right in the centre of the town. It is a waif from a lengthy document. But it chances to be intelligible. It enumerates six plots of land—'merides' it calls them, from a Greek word meaning 'share' or 'division'—which seem to have formed one parcel: each plot is numbered, and the length of its frontage on the public way (*in fronte*), the name of its lessee or *manceps* and that of his surety (*fideiussor*) are added. The frontages of four plots make up 200 ft. (those of the other two are lost), and it has been suggested that the six together made up 240 ft. The depth—which is not stated on the surviving fragment, but was doubtless uniform for all the plots—may then have been 120 ft., and the whole parcel may have covered 120 × 240 ft., that is, a Roman 'iugerum'. It was plainly a piece of town property. The largest 'meris', Plot v, measured only 25 by 40 yds. and no one would care for such a field or farm. Besides, this plot at one end adjoined a 'ludus' or gladiatorial school, and it fronted AD K, *ad kardinem*, on to the street called in surveying language the 'cardo'. The whole land apparently belonged to one lessee who held it from the municipality on something like a perpetual lease.[1]

Here, in short, is the record of an oblong 'insula' in the Roman town of Orange. It is doubtless part of a longer record, a register of house-property in the whole town. Orange, Colonia Iulia Secundanorum Arausio, was a 'colonia' founded about 45 B.C. with discharged soldiers of Caesar's Second Legion. Possibly the register was drawn up at this date; more probably it is rather later and may be connected with a *census* of Gaul begun about 27 B.C. Certainly it was preserved with much care, as if one of the 'muniments' of the citizens. The spot where it was dug up is in the heart of the ancient as well as of the modern town, close to the probable site of the Forum, and the inscription may have been fastened up in all its length on the walls of some public building. If, as is likely, the town owned the soil of the town, the connexion of the inscription with the Forum becomes even clearer. In any case, the town was plainly laid out in a rectangular street-plan. To-day its lanes are as tortuous as those of any other Provençal town.[2] A strange chance reveals what it and many other of these towns must once have been.

[1] For the inscription see Espérandieu, *Acad. des Inscriptions, Comptes rendus*, 1904, p. 497; Cagnat, *Année Épigr.*, 1905, 12; and especially Schulten, *Hermes*, 1906, 1; a convenient English account is given by H. S. Jones, *Companion to Roman Hist.*, p. 22. It has been suggested by Schulten that the blocks were at first divided into plots of 35 ft. frontage, and that the boundaries had become changed in the ordinary course of things before the survey was made. But this seems to carry conjecture rather far.

[2] It has been said to show marks of streets laid out rectangularly, but neither the look of the town itself nor the plans of it seem to me to confirm this idea; compare Lenthéric, *Le Rhône*, ii. 110.

*Timgad* (figs. 22, 23).

From this piece of half-literary evidence we pass to purely archaeological remains, and first to the province

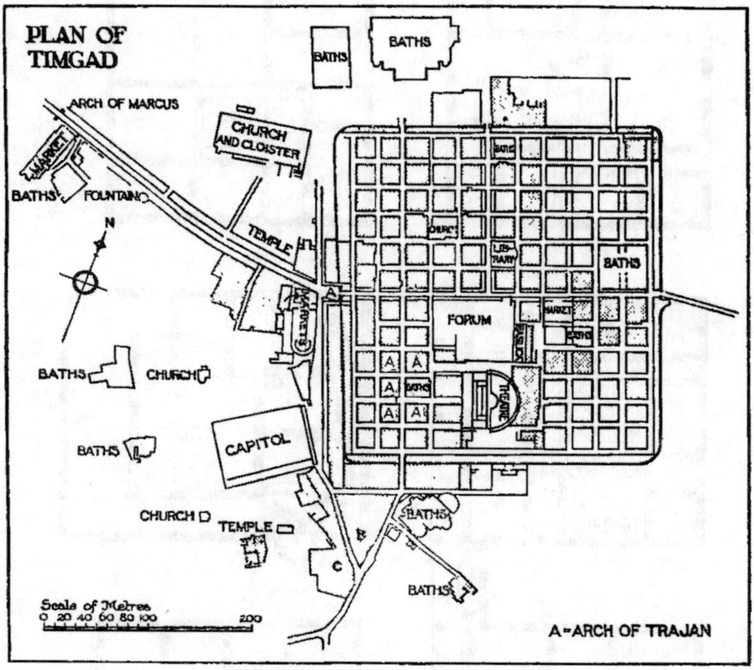


FIG. 22. AFTER CAGNAT AND BALLU (1911). The six 'insulae' marked A are shown in detail in fig. 23. Unshaded 'insulae' are as yet unexcavated.

of Numidia in Roman Africa and to the town of Timgad. The town of Thamugadi, now Timgad, lay on the northern skirts of Mount Aurès, halfway between Constantine and Biskra and about a hundred miles from the Mediterranean coast. Here the emperor Trajan founded in A.D. 100 a 'colonia' on ground then wholly uninhabited, and peopled it with time-expired soldiers from the Third Legion which garrisoned the neighbouring fortress of Lambaesis. The town grew. Soon after the middle of the second century it was

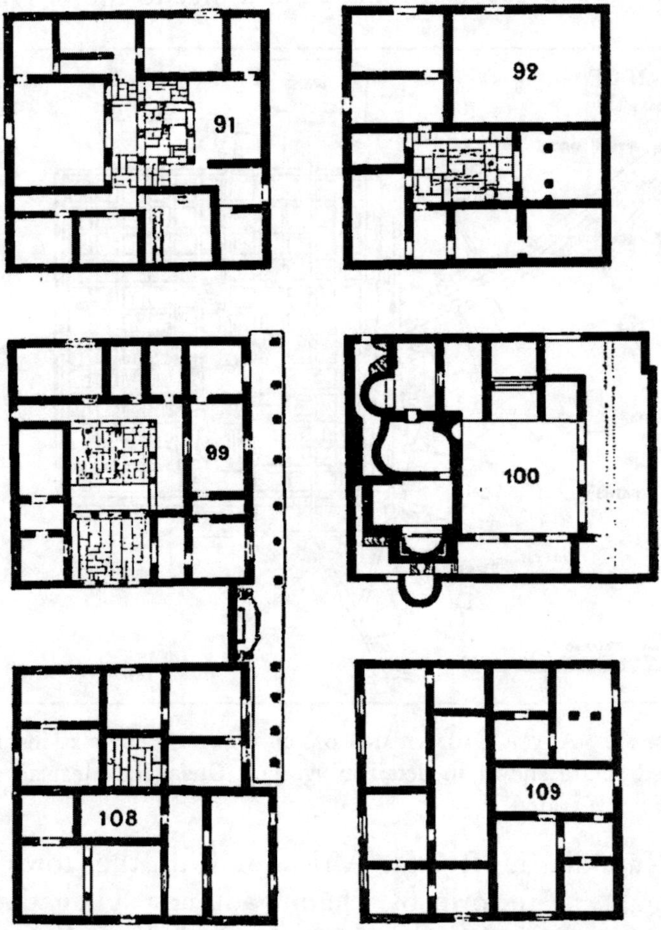


FIG. 23. SIX 'INSULAE' IN S.W. TIMGAD (after Prof. Cagnat). Nos. 91, 92, 99, one house each; 108, 109, 3 houses; 100, Baths. Scale 1 : 600.

more than half a mile in width from east to west, and its extent from north to south, though not definitely known, cannot have been much less. The first settlement was smaller. So far as it has been uncovered by French archaeologists—sufficiently for our purpose, though not completely—the 'colonia' of Trajan appears to have been some 29 or 30 acres in extent within the walls and almost square in outline (360 × 390 yds.). It was entered by four principal gates, three of which can still be traced quite clearly, and which stood in the middle of their respective sides; the position of the south gate is doubtful. According to Dr. Barthel, the street which joins the east and west gates was laid out to point to the sunrise of September 18, the birthday of Trajan.

The interior of the town was divided by streets into a chess-board pattern of small square house-blocks; from north to south there were twelve such blocks and from east to west eleven—not twelve, as is often stated. The possible total of 132 'insulae' was, however, diminished by the space needed for public buildings, though it is not easy to tell how great this space was in the original town. Ultimately, as the excavations show, eight 'insulae' were taken up by the Forum, four by the Theatre, three by the various Baths, one by a Market, one by a Public Library, and one by a Christian church. But some of these edifices were certainly not established till long after A.D. 100 and the others, which must have existed from the first, were soon extended and enlarged. A competent writer on the subject, Dr. Barthel, allows seven blocks for public purposes in the original town, but this seems too little. The blocks themselves measured on the average a square of 70 Roman feet (23 × 23 yards), and may have contained one, two, three, or even four houses apiece, but they have undergone so many changes that their original arrangements are not at all clear. The streets which divided these blocks were 15 to 16 ft. wide; the two main streets, which ran to the principal gates, were further widened by colonnades and paved with superior flagging. All the streets had well-built sewers beneath them.

Trajan's Timgad was plainly small. On any estimate of the number of houses, the original draft of veterans sent there in A.D. 100 can hardly have exceeded 400, and the first population, apart from slaves, must have been under 2,000. This agrees with the figures of Aosta (p. 89). There, 100 acres took 3,000 veterans and their families; here the area is about one-third of 100 acres and the ground available for dwellings may perhaps have been one-sixth. In neither case was space wasted. There was not probably at Aosta, there certainly was not at Timgad, any provision of open squares, of handsome façades, of temples seen down the vista of stately avenues; there were not even private gardens. The one large unroofed space in Timgad was the half-acre shut within the Forum cloister. This economy of room is no doubt due to the fact that the 'colonia' was not only a home for time-expired soldiers, but, as Prof. Cagnat has justly observed, a quasi-fortress watching the slopes of Mount Aurès south of it, just as Aosta watched its Alpine valley. As Machiavelli thought it worth while to observe, the shorter the line of a town's defence, the fewer the men who can hold it. The town-planning of Timgad was designed on other than purely architectural or municipal principles. For this reason, too, we should probably seek in vain any marked distinction between richer and poorer quarters and larger or smaller houses.[1] The centurions and other officers may have formed the first municipal aristocracy of Timgad, as retired officers did in many Roman towns, but there can have been no definite element of poor among the common soldiers.

Such was Trajan's Timgad, as revealed by excavations now about two-thirds complete. The town soon burst its narrow bounds. A Capitol, Baths, a large Meat-market, and much else sprang up outside the walls. Soon the walls themselves, like those of many mediaeval towns—for example, the north and west town-walls of Oxford—were built over and hidden by later structures. The town grew from one of 360 to a breadth of over 800 yds. And as it expanded, it broke loose from the chess-board pattern. The builders of later Timgad did not resemble those of later Turin. Even the *decumanus*, the main 'east and west' street, wandered away north-west in an uncertain curve, and all that has been discovered of streets outside the walls of Trajan is irregular and complicated. A town-plan, it seems, was binding on the first builders of the 'colonia'. It lost its power within a very few years.[2]

### *Carthage* (fig. 24).

It remains to note another example of town-planning in a Roman municipality of the western Empire, which is as important as it is abnormal. Carthage, first founded —though only in an abortive fashion—as a Roman

[1] Ballu detects a 'quartier industriel' in the outer town, but the evidence does not seem to warrant so grand a term.

[2] Boeswillwald, Cagnat and Ballu, *Timgad* (Paris, 1891–1905); see especially Appendix, pp. 339–349; Ballu, *Ruines de Timgad* (Paris, 1897–1911); Barthel, *Bonner Jahrbücher*, cxx. 101.

'colonia' in 123 B.C. and re-established with the same rank by Julius Caesar or Augustus, shows a rectangular town-plan in a city which speedily became one among the three or four largest and wealthiest cities in the Empire. The regularity of its planning was noted in ancient times by a topographical writer.[1] But the plan,

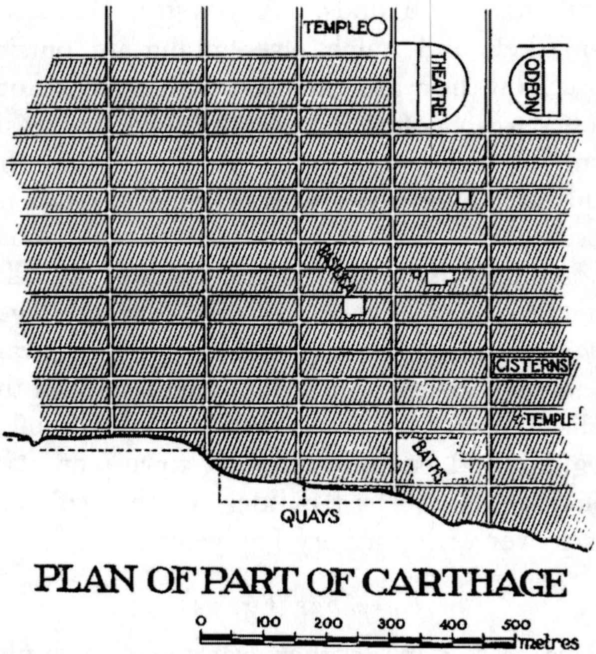


FIG. 24. RESTORED, AFTER GAUCKLER AND DELATTRE.

though rectangular, is not normal. According to the French archaeologists who have worked it out, it comprised a large number of streets—perhaps as many as forty—running parallel to the coast, a smaller number

[1] *Totius orbis descriptio*, 61 (Müller, *geogr. graeci min.* ii. 527); 'dispositione gloriosissima constat . . . in directione vicorum et platearum aequalibus lineis currens' (written probably about A.D. 350).

running at right angles to these down the hillside towards the shore, and many oblong 'insulae', measuring each about 130 × 500 ft., roughly two Roman *iugera.* The whole town stretched for some two miles parallel to the shore and for about a mile inland, and covered perhaps 1,200 acres. Its street-plan can hardly be older than Caesar or Augustus, but the shape of its 'insulae' appears to be without parallel in that age. It comes closest to the oblong blocks of Pompeii and of Naples (pp. 63, 100), and its two theatres also recall those towns. One reason for its plan may no doubt be found in the physical character of the site. The ground slopes down from hills towards the shore, and encourages the use of streets which run level along the slopes, parallel to the shore, and not more or less steeply towards it.[1]

### *Laibach* (fig. 25), *Numantia*, *Lincoln* (fig. 26).

Three or four more ordinary examples chosen at random from provincial municipalities may show the diffusion of town-planning in the western Roman world. One example, from the borders of Italy, may be found just outside the pleasant town of Laibach in southern Austria. Here Augustus in 34 B.C. planted a 'Colonia Iulia Augusta Emona', and recent work of Dr. W. Schmid has thrown much light on its character. The colony was in outline a rectangle of nearly 55 acres (480 × 560 yds.), and was divided up into forty-eight blocks by five streets which ran north and south and

[1] *Carte archéologique et topogr. des Ruines de Carthage*, by Gauckler and Delattre (1 : 5,000); Schulten, *Archäol. Anzeiger*, 1905, p. 77; 1909, p. 190; 1911, p. 246; Audollent, *Carthage romaine* (Paris, 1901), pp. 309, 846. The older accounts of Daux and Tissot seem less trustworthy.

seven which crossed them at right angles; of these forty-eight blocks some must, of course, have been taken up by public buildings. They varied in size: the largest as yet planned (II in fig. 25) measured 170 × 195 ft., or ¾ acre; two others measured 163 × 170 ft.; while one block, which contained one large house not unlike the Silchester 'inn', was 112 × 168 ft. (Plan, II), and the block next it was a trifle smaller. None of the dimensions show any trace of the normal

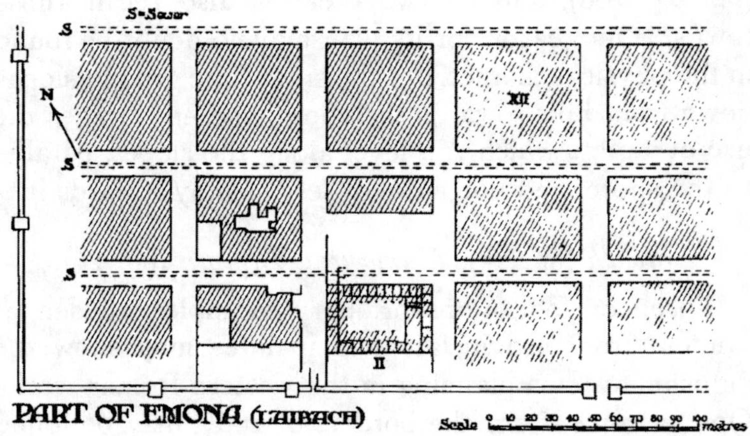


FIG. 25. LAIBACH (from W. Schmid).

120 or 240 ft. (p. 79). The streets were very broad (37–40 ft.); one, which may be the 'cardo maximus', measured as much as 47 ft. across. Beneath the main streets were sewers, in the usual fashion. Round the whole town stood strong walls, reinforced at regular intervals by square projecting towers; the four corners were not rounded but rectangular, after the fashion of Aosta and Turin (pp. 87, 90).[1]

[1] *Correspondenzblatt des Gesamtvereins der deutschen Geschichts- und Altertumsvereine*, April 1912; *Bericht vi der römisch-germanischen*

FIG. 27. BASES OF COLONNADE UNDER BAILGATE, LINCOLN (p. 118).

For a second example turn to a remote corner of central Spain. The town of Numantia was famous in early days for its long struggle with the armies of the Roman Republic. Under Roman rule it was wholly insignificant. Over the débris of Numantine liberty a little Roman town grew up. But it is hardly mentioned save in one or two road-books. Yet it

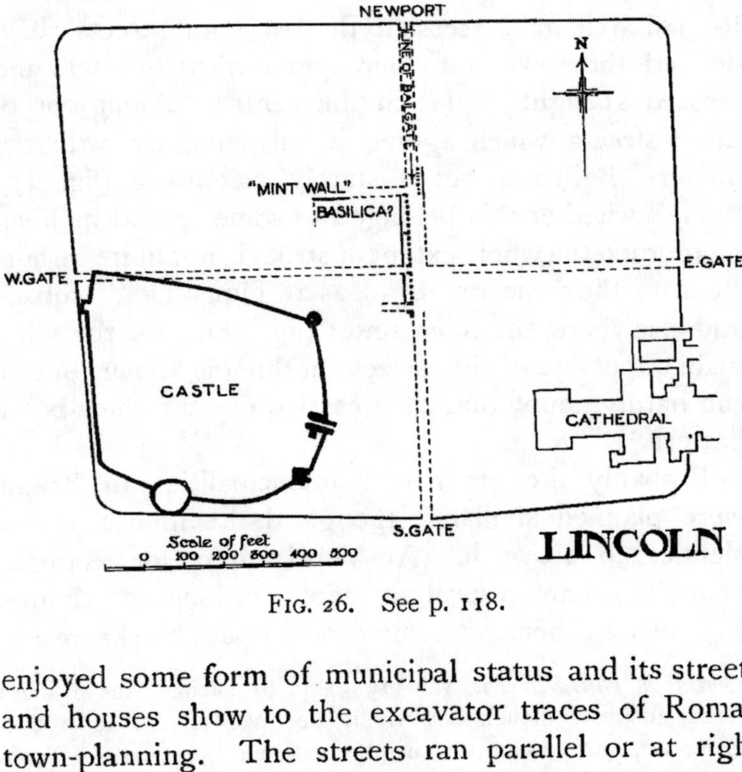


FIG. 26. See p. 118.

enjoyed some form of municipal status and its streets and houses show to the excavator traces of Roman town-planning. The streets ran parallel or at right angles to one another; the house-blocks measured some 50 yds. square.[1]

*Kommission 1910–11*, p. 96. Müllner's *Emona* (Laibach, 1879), p. 19, plate 2, is wholly inadequate.

[1] Schulten, *Abhandlungen der k. Gesellschaft der Wissenschaften zu*

A third example may be drawn from our own country. Lincoln, the Roman Lindum, was established as a 'colonia' about A.D. 75, and the lines of its original area, its 'Altstadt'—for it was perhaps enlarged in Roman times,—can still be traced 'Above Hill' round the Castle and Cathedral (fig. 26). It formed a rectangle just over 41 acres in extent (400 × 500 yds.). Four gates, one of which still keeps its Roman arch, gave access to the two main streets which divided the town into four symmetrical quarters and crossed at right angles in the centre. Along one of these streets, which agrees, if only roughly, with the modern Bailgate, ran a stately colonnade (fig. 27), though whether this belonged to some special building or adorned the whole extent of street is not quite certain. Beneath the same street ran, as at Timgad and Laibach and elsewhere, the town sewer (fig. 28). Of the other main street and of side streets nothing is known, but we can hardly doubt that they carried out the chess-board pattern.[1]

Probably the other four municipalities in Britain were planned similarly, though the evidence is too slender to prove it. At Verulamium (for example) near St. Albans, a local archaeologist long ago claimed to detect a scheme of symmetrical house-blocks, resem-

*Göttingen, phil.-hist. Kl.*, viii. (1905), p. 61, plan 2; the evidence seems adequate though not wholly decisive. The Roman town Emporiae, now Ampurias, in the extreme north-east of Spain, seems to have had a rectangular street-plan, though its Greek predecessor was irregular, *Institut d'estudis catalans, anuari 1908*, p. 185.

[1] *Archaeologia*, liii. 236 and lvi. 371. The plan given by Mr. Fox in liii. 236 represents his own theory, which may be open to doubt.

FIG. 28. LINCOLN. SEWER UNDER BAILGATE.

bling squares very slightly askew. Subsequent inquiry has shown that this scheme was merely or mostly imagination.[1]

[1] J. W. Grover, *Brit. Archaeol. Assoc. Journal*, xxvi. (1870), p. 45, plate 1. The theories of the late Mr. Bellows about the streets of Roman and modern Gloucester were equally astray, though in other ways.

# CHAPTER IX

## ROMAN PROVINCIAL TOWN-PLANS. II

IN the preceding chapters Roman town-planning has been treated in connexion with towns of definite municipal rank, which bore the titles 'colonia' or 'municipium'. The system is, of course, closely akin to such foundation or refoundation as the establishment of a 'colonia' implied in the early Empire, while the no less Roman character of the 'municipium' made town-planning appropriate to this class of town also.

It was, however, not limited to these towns. It appears not seldom in provincial towns of lower legal status, such as were not uncommon in Britain, in Gaul, and in some other districts. Four instances may be quoted from the two provinces just named. In the first, Autun, the town-planning is explained by the establishment of the town full-grown under Roman official influence. Unfortunately, however, little is known of the buildings, and it is difficult to judge of the actual character of the place. In the second case, Trier, we may conjecture a similar official origin. At Silchester, official influence seems also to have been at work, and it is not impossible that the fourth case, Caerwent, may be explained by the same cause. In these two latter, however, it is more important to observe the nature of the towns, which is better known than that of any others in western Europe. For they embody a type of urban life which is distinct from any that occurs in Italy or in the better civilized districts of the Empire, and which illustrates strikingly one stratum of provincial culture.

### *Autun* (fig. 29).

Caesar won northern and central Gaul for the Roman Empire; it fell to Augustus to organize the conquered but as yet unromanized lands. Among many steps to that end, he seems to have planted new native towns which should take the places of old native tribal capitals and should drive out local Celtic traditions by new Roman municipal interests. These new towns did not, as a rule, enjoy the full Roman municipal status; northern Gaul was not quite ripe for that. But they were plainly devised to help Romanization forward, and their object is declared by their half-Roman, half-Celtic names—Augustodunum (now Autun), Caesaromagus (Beauvais), Augusta Suessionum (Soissons), Augusta Treverorum (Trier), and the like.[1] Of two of these, Autun and Trier, we chance to know the town-plans. The reader will notice a certain similarity between them.

Autun stands on the site and contains the stately ruins of the Roman Augustodunum, built by Augustus about 12 B.C. He, as it seems, brought down the Gaulish dwellers in the old native hill-fortress of

[1] Hirschfeld, *Haeduer und Arverner* (*Sitzungsber. der preuss. Akademie*, 1897, p. 1102). Similar hybrid names have been created by the English in India, mostly on the North-west Frontier, where alone they have planted new inhabited sites—Lyallpur, Abbotabad, Edwardesabad, Robertsganj, and the like. But these are almost all small places or forts, and their names represent no policy of Anglicization.

Bibracte, on Mont-Beuvray, and planted them twelve miles away on an unoccupied site beside the river

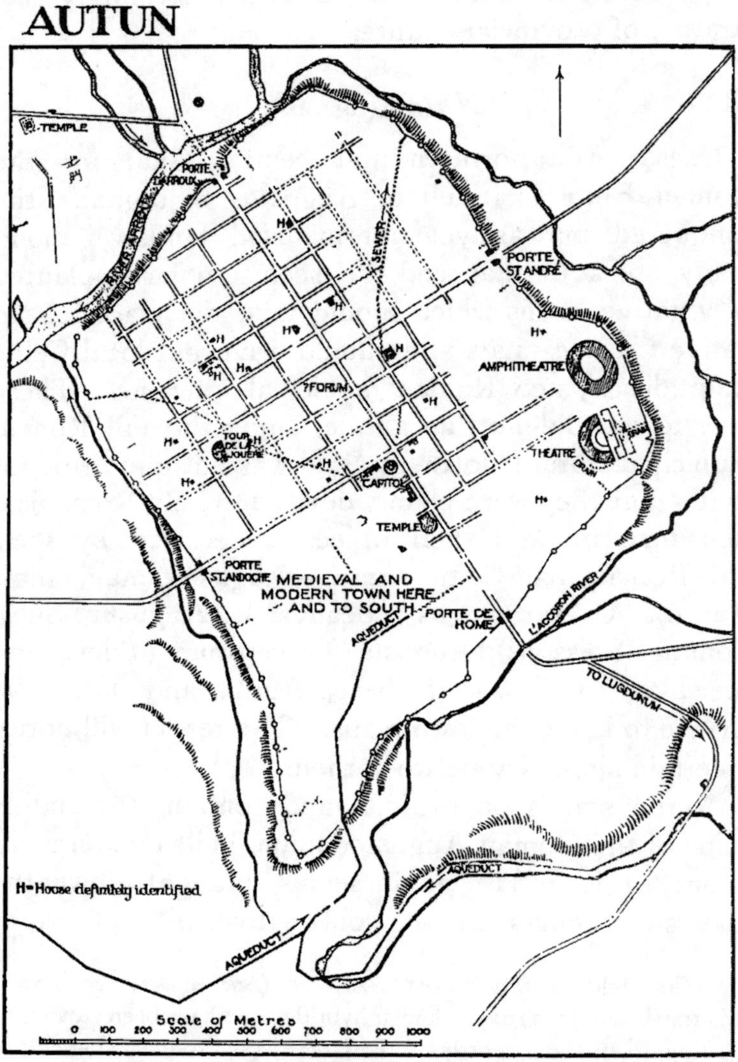


FIG. 29. AFTER H. DE FONTENAY, 1889.

Arroux. The new town covered an area of something like 490 acres—that is, if the now traceable walls and gates are, as is generally thought, the work of Augustus. The town within the walls must have been laid out all at once. Quite a large part of it, perhaps has much as three-quarters, have revealed to the careful inquiries of French archaeologists a regular system of quadrangular street-planning, which may very likely have extended even through the unexplored quarter. The Roman street which ran through the town from south to north, from the Porte de Rome to the Porte d'Arroux, was fronted by at least thirteen 'insulae', and one of the streets which crossed it at right angles was fronted by eleven such blocks. They vary somewhat in size. The larger 'insulae', which lie west of the main north and south street, are oblong and measure about 150 × 100 yds. (say, 3 acres); many smaller ones are more nearly square (98 × 98 or 109 yds., about 2 acres).

But the regularity of the plan is plainly the work of civilized man. When the Celts were brought to live in a Roman city, care was taken that it should be really Roman.[1] Only we may perhaps wonder whether the plan may not have been drawn by Augustus with an eye more to the future than to the present and may have included more 'insulae' than there were actually inhabitants to occupy at once. That was the case certainly in the mediaeval English town of Winchelsea, where the rectangular building-plots laid out by Edward I have in great measure lain empty and untenanted to the present day.

[1] H. de Fontenay, *Autun et ses monuments* (Autun, 1889), pp. 49 foll. and map (1 : 6,250). The existence of a town-plan was first noticed by J. de Fontenay, *Bulletin monumental*, 1852, p. 365, but his map appears to be incorrect and his views generally are based too much on *a priori* assumptions.

### *Trier* (fig. 30).

We may take another example from a northern city, Trier on the Mosel, in north-eastern Gaul (Augusta Treverorum). It was in its later days a large city, perhaps the largest Roman city in western Europe. When its walls were built and its famous north gate, the Porta Nigra, was erected, probably towards the end of the third century, they included a space of 704 acres, twenty-five times as much as the original Timgad, though, it must be added, this area may not have been wholly covered with houses. But it was then an old city. Its earliest remains date from the earliest days of the Roman Empire (A.D. 2), when it was founded, like Autun, on a spot which had (as it seems) never been inhabited before.[1] Of this first beginning we possess vestiges which concern us here. Eight or nine years ago, when the modern town was provided with drainage, the engineers of the work and the Trier archaeologists, headed by the late Dr. Gräven, combined to note the points where the drainage trenches cut through pieces of Roman roadway.[2]

These points yielded a regular plan of streets crossing at right angles, which in many of its features much

[1] Ademeit, *Siedelungsgeographie des Moselgebiets*, pp. 367, 431.

[2] H. Gräven, *Stadtplan des römischen Triers* in *Die Denkmalpflege*, 14 Dec. 1904 (1 : 10,000); the plan has been often copied, as by Cramer, *Das röm. Trier* (Gütersloh, 1911), and Von Behr, *Trierer Jahresberichte*, i. 1908. Compare Barthel, *Bonner Jahrbücher*, cxx. 106. Trier at some time or other became a 'colonia'. When this occurred, is hotly disputed; the evidence seems to me to suggest that it was founded without colonial status and became a 'colonia latina' in the course of the first century (see Domaszewski, *Abhandlungen*, p. 153). I have therefore inserted Trier in this chapter with Autun and not in Chapter VIII with Orange and Timgad.

resembles that of Autun. Thirteen streets were traced running east and west, and eight (Dr. Gräven says seven but his plan shows eight) running north and south. The east and west streets, with two exceptions, lay some 320 ft. from one another. The north and south streets varied, some observing that distance, others being no more than 260 ft. apart. As a result, the rectangular house-blocks varied also in size. The largest seem to be those which fronted a street that crossed the town from east to west, from the Imperial Palace to the Baths and the West Gate, and corresponds roughly with the present Kaiserstrasse. This may well have been the *decumanus*, the main east and west street of the 'colonia', and hence the house-blocks fronting it may have been unusually large (p. 77). One of them, near the Neumarkt, reached the awkward size of nearly 3½ acres (320 × 460 ft.). Others elsewhere were smaller, many measuring 320 × 320 ft., and others again 320 × 245 ft., rather less than 2 acres. In general, the 'insulae' on the east and west sides of the town were larger than those in the centre. The whole has a resemblance to Autun, and is more irregular than writers on Trier are ready to allow.[1]

How many houses may have occupied either a large or a small 'insula' is uncertain; indeed, we know next to nothing of the private houses of Roman Trier. Nor can we fix the number of the 'insulae'. On the west, and still more on the east and south-east of the town, much of the area was not touched by the drainage

[1] Gräven estimated that, except in the central street, all the 'insulae' measured 300 Roman ft. (290 English ft., 88 metres), but his plan suggests rather 100 metres. We need in reality that larger plan which he did not live to complete.

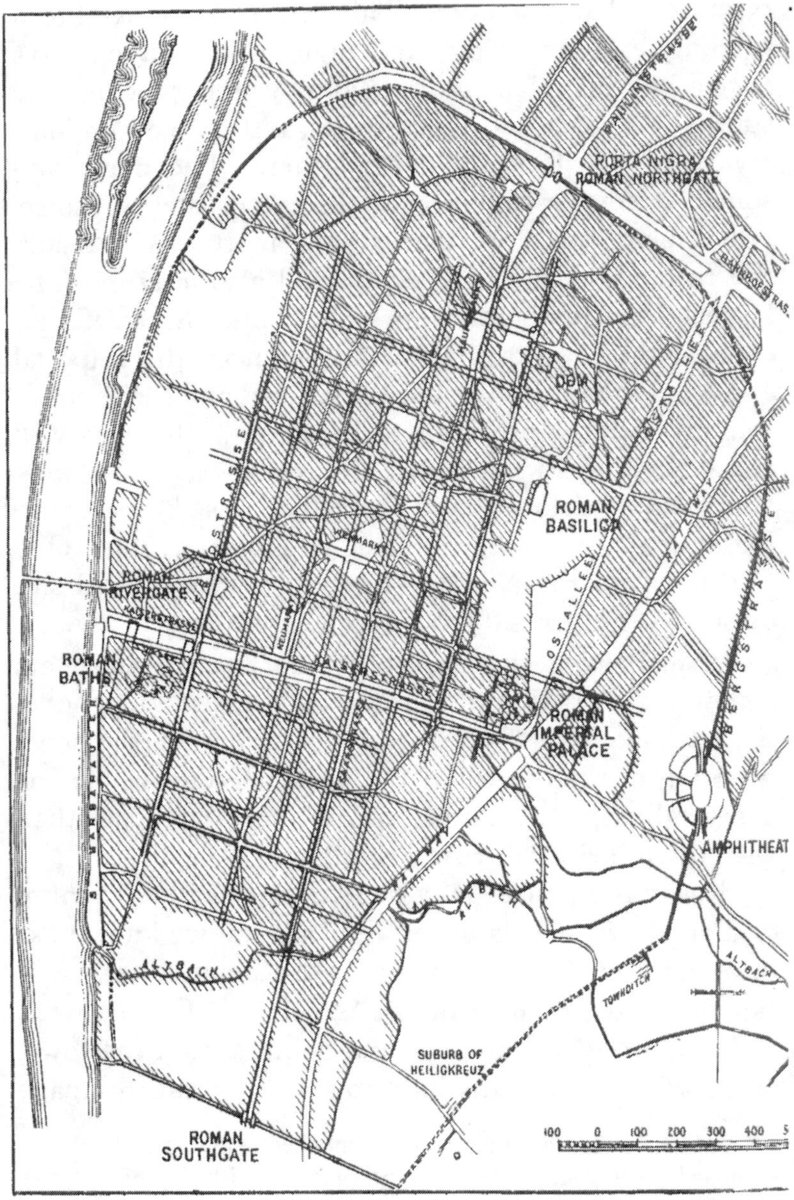


FIG. 30. TRIER. From plan by the late Dr. Gräven.

works and therefore went unexplored. We have proof only of streets and buildings for a mile in length and half a mile in breadth.

Nevertheless we may make some guess at the original area. The streetage itself plainly dates from the original foundation of the Romano-Gaulish town by Augustus. There is, indeed, no other epoch in its history, so far as we know it, when a complete laying out could have been carried through. On the other hand, it is not probable that the first town was a mile long and half a mile wide. Possibly, as an acute German archaeologist has suggested, the small 'insulae' in the south of the town may indicate the line of an original wall and ditch which, like the first walls of Timgad, were overrun later by an expanding town. Certainly, early graves found hereabouts show that this space lay once outside the inhabited area, and similar evidence has been noted both on the north of the town in the Simeonstrasse, and on the west near the Mosel Bridge. If this be so, Augusta Treverorum may have at first covered only 120 or 130 acres; then, as the place spread beyond its original limits, its builders followed more or less closely the lines of the first streets, and, save near the Porta Nigra, continued the chess-board pattern as it was continued at Turin.

### *Silchester* (figs. 31, 32).

Silchester, Calleva Atrebatum (fig. 31), shows a different picture, which is the more interesting because the excavations carried out in 1890–1909 have given us a fuller knowledge of the town than of any other

Roman site in the western provinces.[1] It was, apparently, the old tribal capital of the Atrebates and the county-town of its district in Roman days; though not possessing the full municipal status, it was probably the seat of local government for a consider-

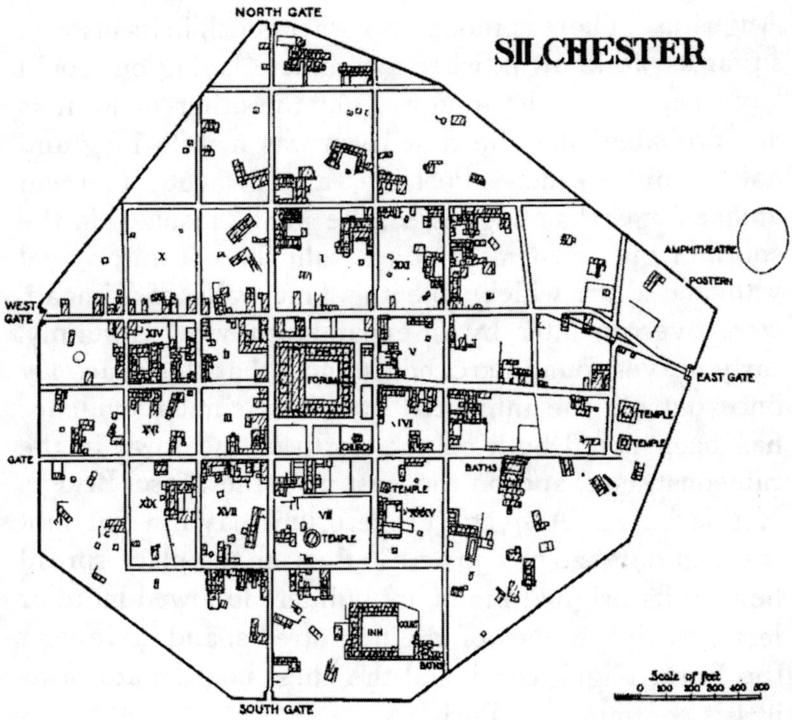


FIG. 31. (For detail see fig. 32.)

able neighbourhood. In outline it was an irregular eight-sided area of 100 acres, defended by a strong stone wall, which was added long after the original foundation. Internally it was divided up by streets

[1] For accounts of the Silchester excavations, see *Archaeologia*, vols. lii–lxii, and *Victoria Hist. of Hampshire*, i. 271, 350; large plan by W. H. St. John Hope (1 : 1,800) in *Archaeol.* lxi.

which, except near the east gate, run parallel or at right angles to one another. Its buildings are: a Forum and Basilica, a suite of public baths, four small temples, a small Christian church, a hotel, and a large number of private houses. Its area is by no means filled with buildings. Garden ground must have been common and cheap, and the buildings themselves do not form continuous streets; they do not even front the roadway in the manner of houses in Italian towns. In these respects Silchester differs widely from any of the examples which we have already considered, so far as their internal buildings are known to us. I will not call it a 'garden city', for a garden city represents an attempt to add some of the features of the country to a town. Silchester, I fancy, represents the exact opposite. It is an attempt to insert urban features into a country-side.

Most of it must have been laid out at once. At any rate, the area of which the 'insulae' numbered X, XXI, XXXV, and XIX form the corners, and the Forum the centre, must have been planned complete from the first. This covers just 40 acres, and is divided into rectangular plots of which the smallest covers a little less than an acre and a half, while the largest fall little short of $3\frac{1}{2}$ acres.[1] Outside this area, the division of the town into 'insulae' is less completely carried through, although most of the streets run straight on as far as the walls, and one or two details may tempt us to think that the division into 'insulae'

[1] The plots are of three sizes, two being 3·4 acres (128 × 130 yds.), six about 2·4 acres (128 × 89 yds.), and six about 1·4 acres (89 × 80 yds.). In the third size the dimension of 240 Roman feet (p. 79) can perhaps be recognized.

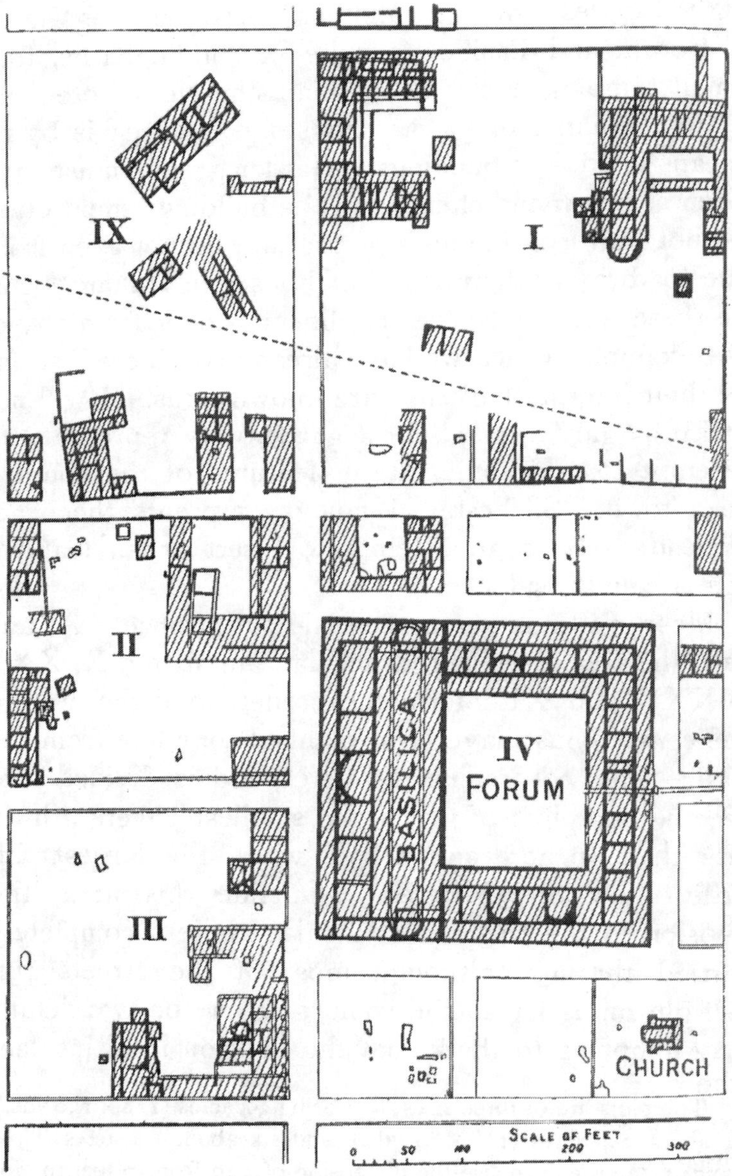


FIG. 32. DETAILS OF FOUR INSULAE, THE FORUM AND THE CHURCH AT SILCHESTER (from *Archaeologia*).

was at some time extended beyond the line ultimately taken by the walls.

But whatever the exact amount of Roman building and Roman street-plan given to Silchester when it was first laid out, the place is not in effect a real town. It is not merely that, as I have said, the houses do not form continuous streets. A glance at the houses will show that they could not possibly be fitted into streets. The types of house here visible are not town houses. They are the types which appear among the 'villas', that is, the landlords' or the farmers' dwellings, up and down the rural districts of Roman Britain and northern Gaul, and the town which they constitute is a conglomeration of country houses. The reverse has taken place of that which we often see to-day in England. Our modern builders and architects had—until perhaps quite recently—only one idea of a small house, the house, namely, which to-day characterizes the monotonous streets in the poorer quarters of our new towns, with its front door and bow window on one side, its offices behind, and its two other sides left blank for other houses to stand against. This is a town house. Yet our modern builders use it, all by itself, in the most desolate country districts. I came across one such not long ago, when driving over a lonely valley in Exmoor. There it stood, with no other house near it, yet with its two sides blankly waiting for the street that ought to form itself to the right and left.

The opposite of this has occurred at Calleva; here the rural house has been used, with scarcely a change, to form a town. We see the Roman street-plan introduced in surroundings which are not properly urban. The outward expression of the civilized municipal system jostles against a provincial and rural life. Here was a premature attempt to municipalize the Briton, which outstripped the readiness of the Briton to be municipalized. Silchester was probably a tribal centre before the Roman came; for awhile it may have remained much the same under Roman rule. But forty years after the Roman Conquest, in the reign of Vespasian (about A.D. 70–85), the Romanization of the whole province appears to have rapidly advanced. It was, indeed, encouraged by the Home Government. Various details suggest that the laying out of Silchester belonged to this very date. But to this the Callevan failed to rise. He learnt much from Rome; he learnt even town-life; he did not learn town-life in its highest form. When his town had been 'haussmannized' and fitted with Roman streets, and equipped with Roman Forum and Basilica, and the rest, he yet continued to live—perhaps more happily than the true townsman—in his irregularly grouped houses and cottages amid an expanse of gardens. The area of Silchester differed little from that of Aosta; its population, if we may judge by the number of dwelling-houses, was hardly as large as that of Timgad.

### *Caerwent* (fig. 33).

I turn lastly to another Romano-British town, Caerwent (Venta Silurum), between Chepstow and Newport in Monmouthshire. It is a smaller town than Silchester. Both towns perhaps began with the same area, 40 or 45 acres. But Caerwent never expanded; it remained not much more than 45 acres within the walls. Land was probably valuable within it; certainly its houses are packed closer, and its garden ground is smaller than at Silchester. Its general type is, however, the same. It has a very similar Forum and Basilica, Temples, an Amphitheatre, and a large number of private houses which resemble closely those of Silchester. It has, moreover, at least in the parts that have been so far excavated, distinct traces of

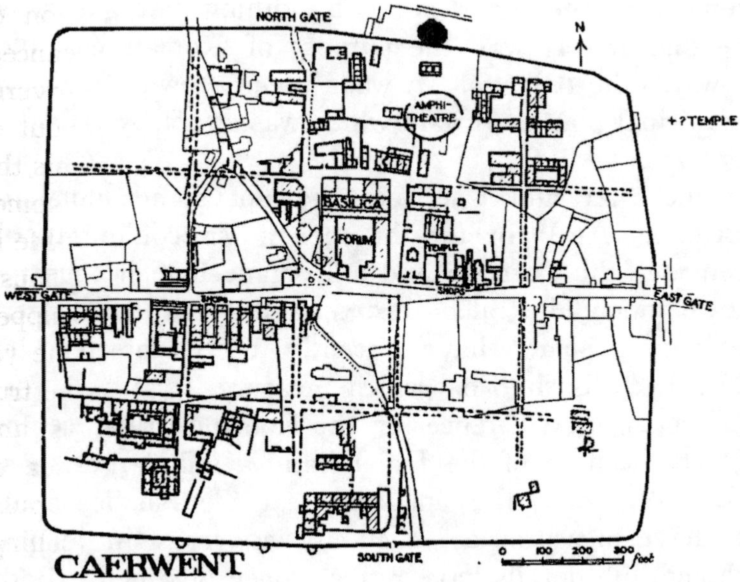


FIG. 33. REDUCED FROM PLAN BY F. KING.

a rectangular street pattern, which, if it was carried through the whole town, would provide (including the Forum) twenty 'insulae'. The size of these blocks cannot be determined with any precision. Indeed, in some cases the houses seem to have encroached on and distorted the street-plan. Probably it would be true to say that the average block covered an acre and a half or an acre and two-thirds.[1] We do not know

[1] The three best defined examples measure about 260 × 260,

enough of the history of Caerwent to do more than guess how this street-plan came to it. Very likely the same process of establishing a Roman-looking town for a local capital was adopted here as at Silchester. Very likely the step was taken in the same period as at Silchester, that is, in the last thirty years of the first century. Its occurrence is significant. Caerwent lay remote in the far west, with nothing but garrisons beyond it. It was the outpost of Roman city life towards the Atlantic. It was the only town of Roman municipal plan in Britain which was swept by Atlantic breezes.[1]

Silchester and Caerwent did not stand alone in Britain. At Wroxeter, the ancient Viroconium, tribal centre of the Cornovii and a Romano-British country-town much like Silchester, though somewhat larger, oblong 'insulae' have recently been detected by Mr. J. P. Bushe-Fox which measure 103 × 126 yds. ($2\frac{2}{3}$ acres). At Cirencester, the Romano-British centre for the canton of the Dobuni and a still larger town than Wroxeter, the 'insulae' near the Basilica seem to have measured as much as 120 yards in length, though full details have not yet been obtained. Both these towns may be ascribed to the later years of the first century and to the same civilizing process as Silchester and Caerwent. As further Romano-British towns are uncovered, we may therefore hope for more

260 × 280, 275 × 275 ft. (1·55, 1·61, and 1·73 acres respectively). The unit of 240 Roman feet (p. 79) does not appear at Caerwent.

[2] Accounts of the Caerwent Excavations, 1899–1910, will be found in *Archaeologia*, vols. lvii–lxii. A good plan of the whole town, from which fig. 33 is taken, was issued in vol. lxii, plate 64, by Mr. F. King, architect to the excavations (scale, 1 : 900).

examples. However imperfectly the inner meaning of town-planning was understood, it was plainly common in the south of Roman Britain.

### NOTE. THE EASTERN PROVINCES.

To complete the survey of Roman provincial town-planning, we must glance briefly at the East. Here towns of Roman origin were few, and of those few scarcely any are well known. But they do not lack interest. For example, take Antinoê, built by Hadrian in memory of his favourite Antinous, on the banks of the Nile. It was a parallelogram more than 3 miles round, which covered an area of 360 acres. Two main streets, each colonnaded, crossed at right angles and cut it into four parts. Of the other streets, nothing cetrain seems to be known. But references to the town in papyri denote four quarters of it by various letters, Alpha, Beta, Gamma, Delta, and distinguish its house-blocks by the term Plintheion with a numeral attached. Thus, a house is described as lying 'in the letter Delta and the Plintheion 7'. Our documents show that there were in Antinoê at least eleven of these Plintheia.[1] It is fairly plain that they are rectangular 'insulae', of either Roman or Hellenic type, while the general fashion of the town and of its monuments suggest a Greek rather than an Italian city.

Another instance may be found still further east, in

[1] *Exploration des ruines d'Antinoe*, by A. C. Gayet (Annales du Musée Guimet, xxvi, Paris, 1897); *Grundzüge der Papyruskunde*, Wilcken, i, pp. 49, 50. Professor A. S. Hunt refers me to the following papyri:—Reinach, 49. 11; Oxyrhynchus, 1110. 9–10 and note there; Brit. Mus. 1164 (c) 12. The numeration of the divisions of the town by letters was borrowed from Alexandria, where the five parts of the city were known as A, B, C, D, E. For plans see the Napoleonic *Description d'Égypte* iv (Paris, 1817), plate 53, and E. Jomard, *Antiquités d'Égypte* (1818), chap. xv.

the land beyond Jordan, at the capital of the Haurân, Bosrâ, anciently Bostra. Little has been achieved in the way of exploration of this site beyond studies of the stately ruins of theatres, palaces, temples, triumphal arches, aqueducts. Little can therefore be said as to the date of its ground-plan. But it was rectangular in outline, or nearly so; and its streets crossed at right angles and enclosed rectangular insulae.[1] The place owes all its greatness to Rome. During the second century it was the fortress of the Legio III Cyrenaica,

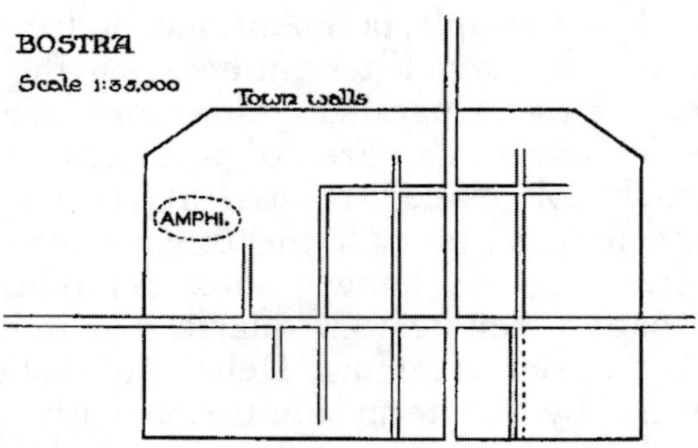


FIG. 34. AFTER BAEDEKER.

which guarded this part of the eastern Roman frontier. About A.D. 225 it became a 'colonia', and perhaps we should date from this the town-plan just described (fig. 34).

This rectangular planning remained long in use in the Eastern Empire. When in A.D. 705 (as it seems) the town of Chersonnesus in the Crimea was rebuilt after a total destruction, it was rebuilt on a symmetrical plan of oblong 'insulae' (25–30 by 60–70 yds. area). Its streets were mean and narrow. But their plan at least was apparently more regular than that of their predecessors.[2]

[1] Baedeker, *Palestine and Syria* (1906), p. 162.

[2] Minns, *Greeks and Scythians*, pp. 493, 508, and references there given.

# CHAPTER X

## Roman Building-laws

Archaeology tells us that the western half of the Roman Empire and many districts in its eastern half used a definite town-plan which may be named, for brevity, the chess-board pattern. It remains to ask whether literature, or at least legal literature, provides any basis of theory or any ratification of the actual system which archaeology reveals. Of augural lore we have indeed enough and to spare. We know that the *decumanus* and the *cardo*, the two main lines of the Roman land-survey and probably also the two main streets of the Roman town-plan,[1] were laid out under definite augural and semi-religious provision. We should expect to find more. A system of town-planning that is so distinctive and so widely used might reasonably have created a series of building-laws sanctioning or modifying it. This did not occur. Neither the lawyers nor even the land-surveyors, the so-called Gromatici, tell us of any legal rules relative to town-planning as distinct from surveying in general. The surveyors, in particular, are much more concerned with the soil of the province and its 'limitation' and 'centuriation', than with the arrangements of any individual town, and, whatever their value for extra-mural boundaries,[2] throw no light on streets and 'insulae'.

[1] See p. 73. [2] Schulten, *Hermes*, 1898, p. 534.

The nearest approach to building-laws which occurs is a clause which seems to be a standing provision in many municipal charters and similar documents from the age of Cicero onwards, to the effect that no man might destroy, unroof, or dismantle an urban building unless he was ready to replace it by a building at least as good or had received special permission from his local town council. The earliest example of this provision occurs in the charter of the municipality of Tarentum, which was drawn up in the time of Cicero.[1] It is repeated in practically the same words in the charter of the 'colonia Genetiva' in southern Spain, which was founded in 44 B.C.; it recurs in the charter granted to the municipality of Malaga, also in southern Spain, about A.D. 82.[2] Somewhat similar prohibitions of the removal of even old and worthless houses without special leave are implied in decrees of the Roman Senate passed in A.D. 44 and A.D. 56, though these seem really to relate to rural rather than to urban buildings and were perhaps more agrarian than municipal in their object.[3] Hadrian, in a dispatch written in A.D. 127 to an eastern town which had lately obtained something like municipal status, includes a

[1] Mommsen, *Eph. Epigr.* ix, p. 9; Dessau, *Inscr. sel.* 6086; 'nei quis in oppido quod eius municipi erit aedificium detegito neive demolito neive disturbato nisei quod non deterius restiturus erit nisei de senatus sententia. sei quis adversus ea faxit, quanti id aedificium fuerit, tantam pequniam municipio dare damnas esto eiusque pequniae quei volet petitio est.' (English translation in E. G. Hardy's *Roman Laws and Charters*, p. 101.)

[2] Dessau, 6087, 6089; Hardy, *Roman Laws*, part 2, pp. 34, 108.

[3] For these decrees, which are practically equivalent at this date to laws, see *CIL.* x. 1401 = Dessau 6043, and de Pachtère in *Mélanges Cagnat*, p. 169.

provision that a house in the town belonging to one Claudius Socrates must either be repaired by him or handed over to some other citizen.[1] Similar legislation occurs in A.D. 224 and in the time of Diocletian and later.[2]

Rules were also laid down occasionally to forbid balconies and similar structures which might impede the light and air in narrow streets, and it was a common rule that cemeteries and brickyards must lie outside the area of inhabitation. At Rome too, efforts were made by various emperors to limit the height of the large tenement houses which there formed the 'insulae'. These limits were, however, fixed haphazard without due reference to the width of the streets; they do not seem to occur outside of Rome, and even in Rome they were very scantily observed.

But in general no definite laws were framed. Probably the municipalities were somewhat closely tied in the administration of municipal property and had to refer schemes for the employment even of the smallest bit of vacant space to the 'patron' or the *curator* of the town. But, apart from the provisions mentioned above, they had no specific rights, that are recorded, against private owners or builders. It was only once, after Rome itself had been burnt out, that an imperial order condemned landowners who 'held up' their ground instead of using it, to forfeit their ownership in favour of any one who offered to build at once.

[1] For the letter of Hadrian see *Bulletin de Corresp. Hell.* x. 111; it is quoted by Bruns, *Fontes,* 1909, p. 200. Compare the *Historia Augusta,* Life of Hadrian, ch. 18.

[2] Mommsen, *Eph. Epigr.* iii, p. 111 and *Ges. Schiften*, i. 158, 263, 371; Liebenam, *Städteverwaltung*, 393.

# CHAPTER XI

## THE SEQUEL

WHAT was the sequel to this long work of town-planning? Two facts stand out distinct. First, the Roman planning helped the towns of the Empire to take definite form, but when the Empire fell, it too met its end. Only here and there its vestiges lingered on in the streets of scattered cities like things of a former age. But, secondly, from this death it rose again, first in the thirteenth century, with ever-growing power to set the model for the city life of the modern world.

I. The value of town-planning to Roman civilization was twofold. It increased the comfort of the common man; it made the towns stronger and more coherent units to resist the barbarian invasions. When, after 250 years of conflict, the barbarians triumphed, its work was done. In the next age of ceaseless orderless warfare it was less fit, with its straight broad streets, for defence and for fighting than the chaos of narrow tortuous lanes out of which it had grown and to which it now returned. The cases are few in which survivals of Roman streets have conditioned the external form of mediaeval or modern towns. We in England tend perhaps to overrate the likelihood of such survivals. Our classical education has, until very lately, taught most of us more of ancient than of mediaeval history, and when our antiquaries find towns rectangular in outline and streets that cross in a Carfax, they give them a Roman origin.

Such a tendency is wrong. Plentiful evidence shows that even in Italy and even in towns where men have dwelt without a break since Roman days, the Roman streets, and with them the Roman town-plans, have far oftener vanished than endured. Rome herself, the Eternal City, uses hardly one street to-day which was used in the Roman Empire. Some few Italian towns, described in detail above, have a better claim to be called 'eternal'; half a dozen in northern Italy retain their ancient streets in singular perfection. Yet even there cities like Padua and Mantua, Genoa and Pisa, have lost the signs of their older fashion. So, too, in the provinces. In the Danubian lands only one town can even be supposed to preserve a few of its Roman streets. In all the once great cities of that region, Sirmium and Siscia, Poetovio and Celeia and Emona, they have wholly gone; you may walk across the sites to-day and seek them in vain in modern street or hedgerow or lane. In Gaul there were many Roman municipalities in the south; there were many towns of lesser rank but equal wealth in the centre and west and north. But we owe our knowledge of their town-plans to an inscription from Orange and to some excavations at Autun and Trier. Cologne and Trier alone, or almost alone, keep Roman streets in modern use, and they are significant. Both became Roman towns in the first century; both held colonial rank; both have lived on continuously ever since and hardly changed their names. Yet both bear to-day the stamp of the Middle Ages, and the Roman streets which they use are small and nearly unrecognizable fragments.

There is, indeed, no law of survivals. Chance—that convenient ancient word to denote the interaction of many imponderable forces—has ruled one way in one place and otherwise in another. Sometimes monuments have alone survived, sometimes only streets, and we can seldom give reasons for this contrast of fates. At Pola, gates, temples, and amphitheatre still tell of the Roman past and the modern town-square keeps so plainly the tradition of the Forum that you cannot walk across it without a sense of what it was. Yet not a single street agrees with those of the Roman 'colonia'. In the Lombard and Tuscan plains, at Turin and Pavia and Piacenza, at Florence and Lucca, the Roman streets are still in use, just as the old Roman field-ways still divide up the fertile plains outside those towns. But, save in Turin, hardly one Roman stone has been left upon another. In the no less fertile plain of the lower Rhone, at Nîmes and Arles and Orange, the stately ruins wake the admiration of the busiest and least learned traveller; of the Roman streets there is no sign.

Britain has enjoyed less continuity of civilization than any other western province; in Britain the survivals are even fewer. In London, within the limits of the Roman city, no street to-day follows the course of any Roman street, though Roman roads that lead up to the gates are still in use. At Colchester the Roman walls still stand; the places of the Roman gates are known; the masonry of the west gate is still visible as the masonry of a gateway. But the modern and ancient streets do not coincide, and the west gate, which has so well withstood the blows of time, can hardly be reached by road from within the city. At York the defences of the legionary fortress have still their place in the sun, but the 'colonia' on the other bank of the Ouse has vanished wholly from the surface, walls and streets together, and the houses of the citizens of Eburacum are known solely by finds of mosaic floors. At Lincoln the Roman walls and gates can easily be traced and one gate rears its arch intact, but the Bailgate alone follows, and that erratically, the line of a Roman street. The road from the Humber, thirty miles north of Lincoln, runs to-day, as it has run for eighteen centuries, under the Newport arch and through the modern town and passes on southwards. That long straight road has given a feature to Lincoln, but it is a feature due to the Roman highway outside the town, not to the streets within it. Lincoln itself is as English as Cologne and Trier are German.

II. But if Roman streets have seldom survived continuously to modern days, if Roman town-planning perished with the western Empire, it has none the less profoundly influenced the towns of mediaeval and modern Europe and America. Early in the thirteenth century men began to revive, with certain modifications, the rectangular planning which Rome had used. Perhaps copying Roman originals seen in northern Italy, Frederic Stupor Mundi now built on a chess-board pattern the Terra Nova which he founded in Sicily. Now, in 1231, Barcelonette was built with twenty square 'insulae' in south-eastern France. Now, too, the 'Bastides' and 'Villes Neuves' of southern France and towns like Aigues-Mortes (1240) were built on similar plans.[1]

[1] For the Bastides and Villes Neuves see Dr. A. E. Brinckmann, *Deutsche Bauzeitung*, Jan.–Feb., 1910, and, for an example, fig. 35. Many of them may be earlier than 1200 (A. Giry, *Bibl. de l'École des Chartes*, xlii. 451), but those with more or less chess-board plans seem later.

Soon after, the chess-board pattern came to England and was used in Edwardian towns like Flint[1] and Winchelsea; then, too, it was adopted at the other end of the civilized world by German soldiers in Polish lands. Cracow, for example, owes to German settlers in the mid-thirteenth century that curious chess-board pattern of its innermost and oldest streets which so

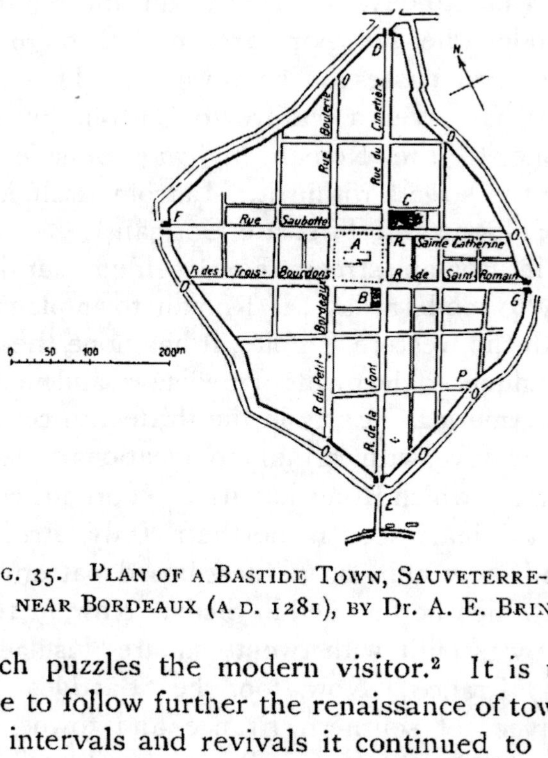


FIG. 35. PLAN OF A BASTIDE TOWN, SAUVETERRE-DE-GUYENNE NEAR BORDEAUX (A.D. 1281), BY DR. A. E. BRINCKMANN.

much puzzles the modern visitor.[2] It is unnecessary here to follow further the renaissance of town-planning. By intervals and revivals it continued to spread. In 1652 it reached Java, when the Dutch built Batavia.

[1] Compare E. A. Lewis, *Medieval Boroughs of Snowdonia*, pp. 30, 61 foll.

[2] So, too, Lemberg. Compare R. F. Kaindl, *Die Deutschen in den Karpathenländern*, i. 178, 293; ii. 304; he does not, however, deal with the actual plans.

In 1682 it reached America, when Penn founded Philadelphia. In 1753, when Kandahar was refounded as a new town on a new site, its Afghan builders laid out a roughly rectangular city, divided into four quarters meeting at a central Carfax and divided further into many strangely rectangular blocks of houses.[1]

But in growing, the old town-planning has passed into a new stage. The Romans dealt with small areas, seldom more than three hundred acres and often very much less. The town-plans of the Middle Ages and even of modern times affected areas that were little larger. Only the last days have brought development. Till the enormous changes of the nineteenth century—changes which have transferred the termination of ancient history from A.D. 476 to near A.D. 1800—the older fashions remained, in town-life as in most other forms of civilized society. Towns were still, with few exceptions, small and their difficulties, if real, were simple. Save in half a dozen abnormal capitals, they had, even in relatively modern days, no vast populations to be fed and made into human and orderly citizens. They had no chemical industries, no chimneys defiling the air, or drains defiling the water. Now, builders have to face the many square miles of Chicago or Buenos Ayres, to provide lungs for their cities, to fight with polluted streams and smoke. Their problems are quite unlike those of the ancients. When Cobbett, about 1800, called London the Great Wen, he contrasted in two monosyllables the ancient ideal of a city with the ugly modern facts.

[1] I have to thank the late Sir Alfred Lyall for a sight of a survey made by English engineers in 1839.

It is not, therefore, likely that modern architects or legislators will learn many hints from plans of Timgad or of Silchester. There are lessons perhaps in the growth of Turin from its little ancient chess-board to its modern enlargement, but such developments are rare. The great benefit to modern workers of such a survey as I have attempted is that it shows the slow and painful steps by which mankind became at last able to plan towns as units, yet inhabited by individual men and women, and that it emphasizes the need for definite rules and principles. Nor is it perhaps quite superfluous to-day to point out how closely, even after the great upheaval of the nineteenth century, the forms of modern life depend on the Roman world.

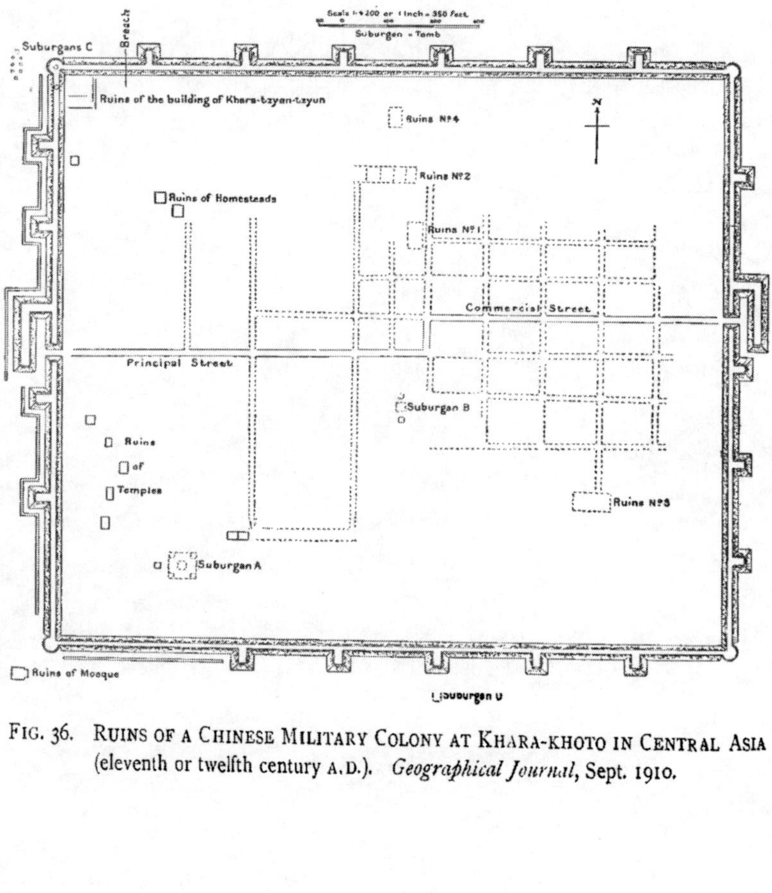


FIG. 36. RUINS OF A CHINESE MILITARY COLONY AT KHARA-KHOTO IN CENTRAL ASIA (eleventh or twelfth century A.D.). *Geographical Journal*, Sept. 1910.

# APPENDIX

## CHINESE TOWN-PLANNING

An essay in ancient town-planning ought to include some account of town-planning in the far east, in China and Japan. Unfortunately, no more than a reference is here possible. Chinese antiquities lie beyond the range of classical scholars, and the particular subject of Chinese town-planning seems not to have been systematically treated by any oriental scholar.

Many towns in China and also in Japan[1] show more or less definite traces of 'chess-board' planning which recall the customs of the Macedonian and Roman worlds. The outlines of such towns are sometimes rectangular, though sometimes wholly irregular as if the sport of local conditions; their streets, or at least their main streets, run generally straight and at right angles to one another and end at symmetrically placed gateways. This is no modern device. Probably it goes back two thousand, or even three thousand, years. The illustration[2] which I give here, in fig. 36, showing one of the Chinese military colonies planted in Turkestan in the eleventh or twelfth century, is selected not as the oldest, but as the best example which I can find of more or less ancient Chinese planning. There seems no doubt that the system itself is very much more ancient than this instance. Even in Japan, which probably copied China in this respect, towns were laid out in chess-board fashion long before the twelfth century; such are the former capitals, Kioto and Nara,

[1] The most accessible plans are in Madrolle's and Murray's Guides. For some notes on Japan I am indebted to Sir Ernest Satow.

[2] From a paper by Col. Kozloff, *Geographical Journal*, Sept. 1910. For the date I have the authority of Sir Aurel Stein.

the latter of which is said to have been founded as early as A.D. 708.

Probably the custom is connected with a very old agrarian system, sometimes known as the 'Tsing' system (from the shape of the Chinese character of that name), according to

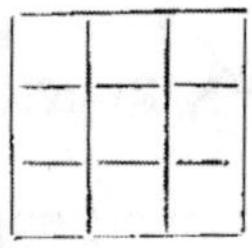

井

which land was divided into square parcels and each parcel was subdivided into nine equal squares. The origin of this system has been ascribed to the twelfth and even to the eighteenth century B.C. About 300 B.C. the philosopher Mencius made it the subject of a financial scheme; of the nine units, eight were to be tilled by eight private owners for their own profit, while the ninth was to be cultivated by the eight men together for the benefit of the State. This Utopian land-tax does not seem to have been actually tried, but it provides confirmatory proof of the antiquity of the agrarian system. It seems that this system may be closely connected with the system of laying out settlements and towns, which developed collaterally with it and produced Chinese town-planning. In China, as at Rome, it would appear that the technical principles on which town and country were laid out were intimately akin.

One item in the Chinese 'chess-board' plan is curiously parallel to a feature which occasionally occurs in Roman towns (p. 88). In many Chinese cities, where the streets are straight and run at right angles to one another, the gates towards which they point are nevertheless not *vis-à-vis*, but the main thoroughfares between the gates make two right-angled turns at some point in their otherwise straight course. Thus travellers do not pass through the town in one continuous straight line, and, as in fig. 36, the east gate is not just opposite

[1] I am indebted to Prof. E. H. Parker and Dr. F. Hirth for suggestions on this point. See F. Hirth, *Ancient History of China* (New York, 1908), p. 296; Dae, *Land-tax in China* (Eighth Oriental Congress, Stockholm, 1889).

the west gate but a short distance to the right or left. The Chinese themselves declare, as my colleague Professor Bullock tells me, that this variation from strict symmetry has a quasi-religious meaning; it is due to the wish that 'good luck' which enters the city should not be able to run straight out at the other end and be lost. A western mind wonders that 'good luck' should only move straight on and might also think that the device which kept in 'good luck' would equally retain 'bad luck'. But the superstition has obviously been invented to explain an ancient custom of forgotten origin.

For ordinary European readers this town-planning of ancient China raises the interesting, if unprofitable, question of the intercourse between ancient China and ancient Europe.[1] The Chinese scholar Terrien de la Couperie once suggested that Chinese civilization was derived from Babylonia somewhere about 2600 B.C. Arguments concerning that period are perhaps dangerous, but it is hardly probable that the Babylonians used town-planning so long ago. Whatever connexion there may have been in ancient times between eastern and western town-planning must be more recent. Our knowledge of these more recent times, however, does not make a connexion seem probable. Not only are the physical obstacles plain enough—the long perilous seas that wash the coasts of southern Asia and the immense deserts and immense mountains of the central continent—but satisfactory proof of real intercourse is wanting. If, as one recent writer emphasizes, the spheres of Roman and Chinese influence, about A.D. 100, were divided only by the waters of the Caspian, if Chinese silk was brought to Rome, and two or three embassies set out from Rome to China or from China to Rome, nothing happened in consequence. Chinese coins are unknown in the Roman Empire, and Roman coins are exceedingly rare in China or anywhere east of Cape Comorin. The Roman geographers, who knew the coasts of Asia to Ceylon, knew little beyond it, and Ptolemy failed to see that the overland route to the far east and the sea-route led to the same country. The early Chinese

[1] F. Hirth, *China and the Roman Orient*; Nissen, *Bonner Jahrb.* xcv.

had no doubt heard of the Roman Empire, just as the Romans had heard of China; such hearsay does not produce any great effect on the civilization of either side. The Chinese doubtless knew much more of Bactria; and Greek, or rather Graeco-Buddhist art, has left abundant traces in the desert cities of central Asia as far as the Chinese Wall. But a town-plan is too complex a thing to travel well. It is plainly more likely that east and west reached their similar results quite independently.

That certainly seems the case with another striking parallel between ancient China and ancient Europe. The Great Wall which encircles northern China and the shorter rampart, lately traced by Sir Aurel Stein, which guarded the road from Pekin to Khotan and Kashgar, are not unlike the fortified frontiers of the Roman Empire. They are earlier than these Roman works. The Great Wall dates from the third century B.C. and the lesser Wall from about 100 B.C.; none of the Roman Walls was begun till nearly 200 years later. But there is no sort of reason to think that the designers of Hadrian's Wall in Cumberland and Northumberland or of the Limes in Upper Germany and Raetia or of any other Roman border rampart were moved by precedents drawn even indirectly from China. The two civilized Empires were faced with the same frontier dangers of invading barbarians; they devised, each for itself, the method of defence by frontier walls. Only, the Chinese defences succeeded; the Roman walls—to the great good of the world—were beaten down.

# INDEX